ENOUGH DOUBLE STANDARD

◇

Hesham Salama

authorHOUSE®

AuthorHouse™
1663 Liberty Drive
Bloomington, IN 47403
www.authorhouse.com
Phone: 1-800-839-8640

First published by AuthorHouse   5/22/2009

ISBN: 978-1-4389-6106-4 (sc)

Printed in the United States of America
Bloomington, Indiana

This book is printed on acid-free paper.

I dedicate this book to all the moderate people all over the world. It does not matter what religion, language, race, or color you are. What matters are your beliefs and thoughts. The important issue is how to be moderate, tolerant, and understanding. When you can give a second thought about any matter, it means you are not prejudiced. When you have a certain point you think you can impose on others, you need to think about it hundreds of times and be certain you are correct. We need to think a great deal more about what we hear and try not to be judgmental. It does not hurt us when we respect others and show them appreciation. What hurts is stubbornness and lack of respect. The rejection of stereotypes is necessary for our success. The things people say and repeat blindly can be devastating to them, their environment, and their community. Tolerance is the best solution for all the problems.

Excessive use of power produces fears, hatred, and aggressions. Our world is already filled up with those harmful features. We do not need any more of them. We need love, cooperation, and coordination among all the people all over the world. There is a common saying nowadays that the world became a small village. Let's give helping hands to one another to promote this village and improve the deterioration that resulted from the world financial crisis. Let's get over our differences and live in peace. Let's respect others and treat them the way we like to be treated.

Hesham Salama

PROPHET ISRAEL AND HIS GRANDSONS

Centuries and centuries ago, Prophet Abraham, who was the father of all the prophets, lived in the Arab land. Prophet Abraham had two sons named Ismail and Isaac. Like their father Abraham, Ismail and Isaac were also prophets. Isaac had a son named Jacob (ב עַקֹ in Hebrew). Jacob was also a prophet who had several followers. Jacob named himself Israel, which means the slave of God. Jacob came to Egypt with his family because of the famines that spread all over the Arab peninsula. Jacob also came to Egypt because his prophet son, Joseph, who was in good terms with the Egyptian Pharaoh. Therefore, Jacob's followers had a great deal of respect from the society.

Hundreds of years later, things became different for Jacob's followers in Egypt. Egypt had a tyrant Pharaoh who was the ruler of the country. Jacob's followers became slaves due to the orders of the Pharaoh. One of the important motives the Pharaoh acted severely towards Jacob's followers was the way they multiplied. He was scared that they might capture the throne of Egypt. The oppressor Pharaoh received a prophecy from one of his people telling him that one of Jacob's followers who would be born that year in Egypt would kill him and end his era.

The Pharaoh believed the prophecy and sent his workers and faithful ones to all the parts of Egypt to kill each newborn boy. The Pharaoh's followers listened to his orders and killed every male child born that year. God's will was stronger than the Pharaoh's. God revealed to Jochabed, the mother of the child who was meant in the prophecy to end the Pharaoh's oppression to put him in casket and throw him in the Nile. The child in his box was picked up in the Pharaoh's palace. The pharaoph's wife, Asia, loved the baby, considered him to be her son. Asia persuaded the Pharaoh to keep him alive. God's mercy conquered the will of people. The child refused to let any woman feed him. His sister was wandering around the palace to make certain he was alright when she overheard some chattering. The sister entered the palace wondering what was happening. She was informed that the baby refuses to eat. His sister said she knew a good lady who could feed him. She brought her mother who was a success feeding her baby.

The Pharaoh raised the baby who was going to put an end to his life later. The baby was Prophet Moses who was the prophet of the Jews. When Moses grew up, he could fulfill the prophecy that the Pharaoh was terrified of. Nowadays, it seems that Prophet Israel (Jacob)'s grandchildren have a prophecy, which says that the Palestinian children will be the reason of their destruction and removal from Palestine, which they call Israel now. The strange issue is that they act cowardly and brutally and that exceeds what the Pharaoh had done with their great grandfathers many centuries ago. The Israelis ignore the fact that God's will and promises always come true, no matter how severely and aggressively they resist such promises. However, they do their best to murder every Palestinian child whenever they get a chance.

THE BUSH ADMINISTRATION AND MUSLIMS

What a cruel world we live in! What an unfair humanity that always sides with the strong against the weak! How rude is a world that always says "Israel has the right to defend itself" and never makes a similar statement about Palestinians! How wonderful to Israel was Bush and his always double standard administration! The Bush's mean administration never hid its real harsh and disgusting feelings towards Arabs and Muslims. You do all that then you deny you are launching a war against Muslims and Islam! You are liars! Absolute liars!

Thanks to President Bush and his spreading and marketing of the idea that every Muslim is a terrorist and a mobile bomb that can explode and destroy all the people around him or her. One day, I watched an Indian movie for Amitabh Bachchan. The movie was about the Pakistani-Indian differences and disputes. During the movie, the two sides had a series of wars. Then, they had some negotiations. An American group was taking part in the negotiations. The Americans tried to bring them to an agreement that prevents any futures wars. Batchchan replied that when Americans lost the two towers of the World Trade Center in Spetmber 11, 2001, America reacted by destroying Afghanistan and Iraq. Batchchan added that India has power to do the same with the ***Muslim Terrorists*** of Pakistan and can destroy them too. This gives the world the impression that Muslims are violent and aggressive. Hence, the victorious Bush and his administration imposed a negative picture about Muslims. They made Muslims seem as usurpers of others' rights and lands. Moreover, the Bush administration dealt and made most of the other non-Muslims all over the world picture Muslims as people with no rights even if they were oppressed and disrespected by any other counterpart.

If we adapt Bush's idea about Muslims and think of the Pakistani who defends his land and rights as a terrorist, we will think the same way of the Palestinian child who throws stones at the Israeli soldiers to defend himself from the tank and the weapons that are always aimed at him or her. You know what, the real problem is not in the grown up people who already had the wrong idea about Muslims. The problem is in the children and teens whom their families, teachers, and society teach to be racist, haters, and rejecters of Muslims.

Amitabh Batchchan, representing India in that movie, considered America's reaction to 9/11 as a model to follow all the time with Muslims and Arabs. The little boys and girls will naturally follow the same procedures towards Arabs and Muslims in their present and future. Muslims and Arab children will respond the same way towards those other children. This way, the coming generation will be more than what we suffer from today. The racial discrimination between Whites and Blacks in America will come back but with different measurements. This coming racial discrimination will rely mostly on religion, ethnicity, and race. Nobody knows if anyone will rise up and say that is wrong and enough. It might take centuries for that if it happens. Before this occurs, many lives will be lost from both sides.

Secretary of State Condoleezza Rice, as it was always her lovely habit, kept saying Hamas has to stop. Why don't you ask Israel to stop it is continual offensive just to allow human aids for the civilians? Today is the 2ⁿᵈ of January, 2009. The former National Security Advisor, Zbigniew Srzezinski, stressed the cruelty of the Bush administration by saying that the world was a lot safer before Bush. In his statement about the Mideast War, which has been taking place for several days the moment of writing these lines, Srzezinski said the Iraq war should not have erupted in the first place. He also added, with Rice policy, the US policy is totally bankrupt. A peace settlement is a priority.

What a hero is Muntadar al-Zeidi, who threw his shoes at Bush! He was correct when he said that was for orphans, widows, and oppressed people. What a real brave statement! Bush is the one who called Muslims 'fascist' and called for 'crusades' against them. He left the Zionists do whatever they want and kill innocent Arabs and Muslims. Why do you see them as your enemies? Even before 9/11 and before you got elected, you were siding with Israelis against Arabs? You did not say a good word about Arabs. Congratulations Mr. President for eight years of indifference about Arabs, Muslims, and Middle Eastern people. I hope you are satisfied now with your cruelty and inhumanity. What a cruel president who knows nothing about mercy or respect of the human soul! How happy are you now with the people of Gaza being killed, injured, insulted, and humiliated? For you, Arafat was a terrorist but Sharon, Olmert, Ehud Barack, Livni are people of peace. What peace?! Do you think the one who defends his or her land is a terrorist and the one who attacks others, demolish their houses, and leave them without shelter is the peacemaker? What a wonderful standard! You do not have to defend Palestinians, Arabs, or Muslims. However, as a president of the largest and strongest nation of the world, you need to be objective and keep your personal feelings of hatred, aggression, and lack of respect towards Arabs and Muslims aside.

Gaza is without electricity. The city is totally dark. The people there cannot get more than just one small bag of bread, no matter what their family members' number is. Where is humanity? Where is your justice, Secretary Rice? No wonder again, you support the cruel and rude Israeli action. Aren't you the one who were upset because President Carter did not use power against Tehran during the hostage crisis and changed your party as Democrats are not fond of using power like Republicans who see themselves as mavericks all the time?

No wonder Republicans talked about nothing other than how Senator John McCain is a maverick. In turn, the mavericks have to choose a good maverick who follows the same steps of the maverick hero President, George W. Bush. Then, the new chosen Republican maverick continues the invasions and aggression against civilizans under the false pretence of bringing democracy to them. McCain, in his campaign used strong harsh language saying Hamas wished he would not get elected because they knew how tough he was going to be with them. Of course, how else should a maverick talk?!

THE INTENDED DEMOCRACY

Since when does democracy occur by bombing, oppression, and aggression? President Bush and his administration pretended to bring democracy to Afghanistan and Iraq, didn't they? What a wonderful democracy when they impose puppet presidents and rulers on the people of both countries such as Hamid Karazi, Jalal Talibini, and Nouri al-Maliki? No matter what they say about the elections in both countries, who can believe them after the false intelligence information and the mission accomplished task in Iraq, which nobody knows when it is going to be accomplished? Moreover, no one can tell if it will ever be accomplished or not.

The intended false democracy created new expressions such as 'friendly fires.' Look at the dozens of people who were killed in 2002 while celebrating a wedding in Afghanistan, and were said, they were mistaken for a terrorist gathering. What can millions of apologies do to those and their families? Will they bring them back to life? Will they get the orphans a new father and mother? Will they live with that apology and cash it out from the bank? Even the money of the whole world, which they can get nothing from, won't be enough and will never be an exchange for the damage and loss they had. Will those apologies bring the wife and kids of the Iraqi whom he lost when his car was bombed by a 'friendly fire?!'

The fact is this cruel and rude world always finds excuses for its wickedness, recklessness, and cowardliness nowadays. Our world always invents excuses for the Israeli leaders for their aggressiveness and impoliteness. The Israeli leaders are nothing but a bunch of cowards and idiots, who believe they are superior to the rest of the human race. Unfortunately, the Israeli leaders always worsen the picture of the Israelis and the rest of the Jews all over the world, who are moderate and objective.

I have nothing against the religion here but against the practices of Israeli leaders such as Olmert, Ehud Barack, and Tzipi Livni. It seems these people have learned their ethics, if they have any, in the school of hatred. They are the hatred itself, and even hatred, can be their student. What the hell are they doing? Why don't they do that, and even a lot more than that, with the approval of one part of the world and the sympathy of the second part, who always sees` Israelis as victims, and they have the right to do whatever they want and use the whole world to get all what they want because of what they say about the holocausts and concentration camps? Isn't what they are doing at the moment, and have been doing and practicing for so many years and decades, worse than what Hitler had done?! They still accuse others of being Nazis and they are the Nazis.

Israelis proved, and continue to prove every day, that they cannot be trusted because they never respect their treaties, which was their issue with Yasser Arafat. Every time before a due date to surrender from a piece of Palestinian land, according to the treaties and peace agreements with the Palestinians, they create some faction and instability in the region. In turn, Israelis refuse to surrender and do what they were to do. Israeli leaders always pretended that the Palestinian riots and aggressions that made them act in a similar way. Sharon was clever at that game and then Olmert followed the same style. Livni is the mistress of all those as she is even more aggressive and full of disrespect towards Arabs and Muslims. Look at what they do and how they tactic their shrewd policy. Instead of applying the peace agreements, they held security meetings with the Palestinians, wasting the times, consuming the efforts, and diverting the attentions from what they should and have to do, deceiving the world who usually sympathizes with them against Palestinians, Arabs, and Muslims.

THE MUSLIM PHOBIA

President Bush and the Israeli leaders had a great deal to do with the spread of the devastating and horrible picture about Islam and Muslims. Their aggressiveness and strikes against the Muslim world always came under the pretence of protection and security. They made the world a cruel place. They blamed Palestinians who explode themselves and say they are terrorists. They said they are cowards. No my dear leaders, you are the cowards. Yes, you are the cowards.

Those people who exploded themselves had not done it for the sake of pleasure. No, those Palestinians were desperate. How do you imagine people whose family was taken out of their homes at a late hour in a cold night in their Pajamas, underwear, bared of shoes or slippers? Then, their homes get either bombed by the F-16 or flattened to the grounds by bulldozers. Should they applaud to Israel and the Israeli leaders? Probably they should. In fact, they should compose a great national anthem for Israel and its cruelty and wickedness. Israel is a state which defies the world community and always gets away with its inhuman measurements really needs to be saluted and supported to do more and more. Go ahead, my dear Israel. You have the support and blessing of America all the time. President Bush, in his weekly radio address, stressed the statement we said earlier, repeated, and learned by heart that "Israel has the right to defend itself." What a wicked person is that president! He and Condoleezza Rice insist on ending their miserable era with showing more racism and lack of respect towards other human beings represented by Palestinians, Arabs, and Muslims.

THE LANGUAGE OF DECEPTION

The Bush administration has been an absolute failure in everything. However, this administration's members are proud of themselves, their failures, and wickedness. In a CNN interview, Daniel Levy, a Middle East strategist criticized the Bush administration's officials because they do not address Palestinians and deal with them as human beings, the way they deal with Israelis. The racist administration is glad to show continual contempt to this race. The cruel staff is not ashamed of themselves. Their highness and majesties deny their double standard in our age of the Internet, satellites, cables, and mass media. The rude ones are satisfied as they strongly believe they are mavericks. It is true. They are mavericks in ignorance. They are dumb in their thoughts, recklessness in their decisions, and thoughtlessness in their measurements.

Condoleezza Rice, according to Daniel Levy, used the same language today, which she had used almost three years ago referring to the war between Israel and Lebanon. The maverick, Rice, said she was not to go to the Middle East or negotiate. She added that she and her administration needed a cease fire as soon as possible. Her boss earlier gave Israel the green light to go ahead and kill the innocent Palestinians. How can a decent human being become indifferent about human souls like that? How can Bush, who is supposed to be a world leader, act this way? He just went to spend a vacation in his Texas ranch cheering up for his nice friends, the Israeli leaders, and dumb the innocent Palestinians. After that, Mr. President, you cannot deny you are going on your war against Islam, directly in Iraq and Afghanistan, and indirectly in Palestine. Bravo Mr. President. Cheers!

The United States, who was famous of defending human rights and human beings, is defying the simplest human rights. Bush is just condemning Hamas. What a great statement! Bush and his administration created more terrorists all over the world. Their hatred of others brought more hatred to the country, which is a reaction for their action. They planted evil. Therefore, they produced more evil. The hatred the Bush administration has from the majority of the people all over the world is not a surprise. It is more than natural. Do you think Mr. President; it is a co-incidence that people, in many countries and all over the world are curious to know what kind of shoes Zeidi threw at you? No, it is not a co-incidence at all. It is the harvest of what you have grown and done during full eight years of racism, recklessness, and indifference. You really deserve a great deal more, don't you?!

Look at the pictures of the young innocent children of Gaza. What have they done? Go ahead and blame it on Hamas and Palestinians. Go ahead and keep defending your spoilt child, Israel. Go on and on, Mr. President. Nothing else can be expected from a racist rude person like you. I said it a lot and I am repeating it. Dictators are cursed in history, and you are one of these dictators. You are so proud of yourself and the destructions you made to humanity. You think your wicked deeds are achievements, Mr. Achiever. You are the achiever and the 'decider.'

DEMOLISHING MOSQUES

The Israelis have been demolishing mosques in Gaza and all over Palestine over the heads of Muslims. It does not matter to you that these mosques are sacred places for Muslims. What will you do and say if the opposite was happening and the Muslims were demolishing churches or Jewish temples? Will you have the same response and say Arabs and Palestinians have the right to defend themselves? Of course not, President Bush! The lousiness of your miserable era and two terms is a disgrace. The American people are paying the price very expensive for their wrong choice twice. However, many Americans are still proud of you and I don't know why. Maybe one of those brilliants can stand up and explain his or her glorious magnificent point of view. I assure you those like you because of just one thing; they are as racist as you are. That is all your qualifications for those who love you deeply. You achieved their goals of contempt and disrespect towards others. You honestly accomplished your mission in that matter. Bravo Mr. President and racist people; ***Mission Accomplished.***

What a great qualification is it just being racist and disrespectful?! You guys who are fond of Bush are wonderful. What you are doing with your blind and continual support does nothing to America but makes other peoples see you as disreputable. We should mourn the days of good reputations. The moderate world does not trust anything comes from America any more. We hope President Obama does not follow the same line and fix the damage. We hope he does not disappoint us. We hope the talks and rumors about him, showing him as Muslim, does not make him turn his back to the Muslim and Arab Worlds to satisfy Israel. We hope he does not become a second George W. Bush. Hope is what we can do as the leaders of the world control us, force us to live miserable eras we do not like or appreciate, and make our life as hard as hell.

I invite the people who like to blame Arabs for every horrible act to go back and do some reading. Read some history. See how the Jewish state of Israel was established before you say we are terrorists. In fact, insisting on making false and baseless accusations is the terrorism itself and the one who insists on it is a terrorist. After you do some reading, researching, and considerable thinking, answer this question: Where was the state of Israel before 1948? Nowhere! Israel is a new invention, invented, composed, and created by America and England. Israel cut a piece of land from the Palestinians, kicked them out of their homes, murdered them, hit their women and children, and stabbed pregnant women with their daggers in their stomachs to kill them and their unborn babies. I have an American friend who once told me that he is always against Arabs and Muslims and he supports Israel all the time. When I asked why, the answer was unclear at all. I am writing this to explain an important matter to him and to all the moderate people who like to know what is really going on. In order to judge other people, you should first be knowledgeable of what is happening. Don't just go on your accusations without having the simplest ideas about anything. It is totally wrong to give yourself the right to offend others without any base of knowledge or experience.

I am Egyptian and I know how Israel acts. We had four wars with Israel. The first war was when Israel with the help of America and Egnland usurped the land of the Palestinians in 1948. The second war was in 1956 when England, France, and Israel attacked and bombed the Egyptian state of Port Said. They made it like Gaza and even much worse. The 1956 triple attack on Port Said was a reaction of an important announcement of the late Egyptian President Gamal Abdel Nasser. Abdel Nasser nationalized the Suez Canal. Nasser said the Suez Canal is Egyptian. It is in the Egyptian land and it is ours. England, France, and Israel did not like the announcement and demolished the houses of Port Said on the heads of its people, the same way Israel has been doing for decades now with Palestinians.

The third war was in 1967, which is known as the six days war or whatever they like to call it. In that war, Israel did the same aggressive acts she does now in Palestine, demolished the three states overlooking Suez Canal: Port Said, Suez, and Ismailia. The people of the three states, who were not killed in the horrible Israeli offensive, had to leave their homes for eight years. In fact, only some of them were able to return home after eight years and it took the others longer to go back. They were scattered in all the other states and governorates of Egypt. That is why, we Egyptians, feel the pain and loss of Palestinians strongly. Their suffering is hard to imagine or describe. They sacrificed a lot, and after that President Bush asks Hamas to stop firing its rockets at Israel. You have never been fair or moderate Mr. President. You could still do a great deal in your last few days of presidency but you are not interested as you always talk down about those people. How come you expect them to like or respect you? We are the ones who can make people love or hate us. Look at all the demonstrations in America and the moderate world, which ask Israel to stop. However, you and Rice are giving us your invaluable statements about the 'durable and sustainable cease fire.' ***Lord Have Mercy!***

The fourth Egyptian war with Israel was in October 1973. Egypt won that war. It was in the era of the Egyptian late President Anwar Sadat. The 1973 war conquered the myth of the Israeli invincible army. It was a great victory for all Egyptians, Arabs, and Muslims who felt relief after teaching Israeli leaders a good lesson that Arabs do not give up their lands for any aggressor. It was an indicator of the return of harmony and respect between the Arab people and their armies.

Another fact the readers should know, if they do not already know about, Israelis defied all the human rules and war conventions and killed the Egyptian captives after the 1967 war. They defied the whole world and went on their corruption. The Israeli leaders who call themselves peacemakers found it too much to leave the Egyptian War Prisoners alive. They should have respected them and treated them in a human manner. On the contrary, they denied them their right to live, the same thing they do with Palestinians now and have been doing since 1948. Israelis tied the Egyptian prisoners of wars with ropes, ordered them to lie down on their stomachs, and shot them. However, Egyptians were forgiving and went on the road of peace but Israelis do nothing to show their respect for that fragile peace.

Today is January 3, 2009, and the Israeli tanks have entered Gaza. The damage the Israelis have done, the killing the Israeli butchers have committed, and the murders against humanity the Israeli war criminals have executed were not enough for you and them, Mr. President. Don't you and they think your ***Mission*** should have been ***Accomplished*** before reaching that extent?! What can I say?! You, Rice, and Livni are involved in such horrors so it can never be any better. It cannot be.

An Israeli army spokeswoman named Avital Leibovich said it was going to be 'a lengthy operation.' Why not as long as you are the one who gives them the green light and the continual blessing Mr. President?! You are their savior and protector. Yes, you are. You are the enemy of Muslims and Arabs and you are the one who started that enmity after all the love and support they gave you before your first term, which you don't deserve at all.

The liar Israeli spokeswoman said they do not target civilians. In this age of satellites and the Internet, the unrespectable spokeswoman lies to the world that can see their violence, lying, and destruction the moment it happens. Again, ***Mission Accomplished!*** Israel also says it is launching a widening war on Hamas. It is a widening war on Muslims and Islam, not just on Hamas. Moreover, Israeli officials say their war will last for several days. Wasn't the damage you have done enough, you cowards and merciless? However, I have to be honest and say that Israel was very nice. They announced that Israel allowed many Palestinians with foreign passports to flee the country. Thank you my dear Israel. You are very kind-hearted. Bravo Israel for your rudeness and defiance towards the whole world. You think you are a country above any laws, constitutions, and norms. What a rude country you are?! Bombing people from air, land, and sea with your F16, heavy artillery, and boat guns is obvious to the whole world. Bravo idiots!

Again Israel proved to be nice by announcing Israel was "not to occupy Gaza." Israeli officials talk as if it is always their right to corrupt on earth, kill, destroy, and rape…etc. That is nothing more than an act of cowards supported by cowards. Israel started it is cowardly war with "a week of aerial bombardment." Aerial bombardment is said to be against Hamas. In fact, it is against all Palestinians. The brave Israeli fighters have the newest arms, goggles, and capabilities while Palestinians have nothing. Do you see how wonderful heroes Israelis are? They believe killing hundreds of innocents collectively is an act of bravery, which is a natural cowardly case.

The simplest rule of balance if you accuse Hamas or Palestinians to be cowards, they are not. Israelis are the cowards. If they want people to face them, those other people should have the same amount of arms and power. Bush also insists ending his era with the worst relationships he can ever have. He insists on his radio address to say Iran and Syria helping terrorism. No wonder Israel insists that it needs more time to achieve its goal. It is splendid goal is to wipe Palestinians and eventually Arabs off earth. President Bush is helping a great deal in such an achievement. Listen to the sounds of guns and how the Israeli soldiers are happy and some of them laughing sarcastically as if they were on a hunting trip. They are real hunters who hunt innocent human beings.

No wonder again how Bush is a nice president as he asks Australia to take some Guantanamo Bay prisoners there. He thinks the Guantanamo Bay detainees are his slaves and he has the right to decide their destiny. Moreover, he is trying to force other countries to hold them in their homelands as prisoners. What does he think about himself, the Lord of the Universe?!

CONTINUAL CRUELTY

The US State Department announced it is working towards a cease fire that does not allow Hamas to fire at Israel. Why don't you also work towards a cease fire that does not allow Israel to fire at Palestinians? The nice humane Israelis drop leaflets on Palestinians' houses and residencies advising them that Israel is going to fire at them and bomb their houses. The butcher Israeli Minister of Defense, Ehud Barak, said that Israelis are men of peace and they know that everyone has the right to live? Why in the world don't you let Palestinians have their simplest right to live and leave them the hell alone in their houses? You order them to leave their houses? Where in the world will they go? You are trying and doing your best to let them go to the Egyptian borders and ask for political refuge. It does not mean anything else. You use the peace agreement you have with Egypt as Egypt respects this agreement but you know nothing about respect of agreements and treaties. You are traitors because you never respect your word. Where are your ethics and manners? You lost them a long time ago when you invaded and occupied Palestine. You are usurpers of land, homes, and innocent lives. You always enjoy killing innocents with cold blood, you cold people. In spite of all that, the world community is silent and the United Nations (UN) is doing nothing more than talking and talking. When the UN does something, it condemns Palestine. When a peaceful agreement is about to be reached, it is blocked by the United States as usual who challenges all the moderate countries, peoples, and organizations with and without a reason all the time. This is not a strange situation. We still have a fairly recent example signified by defying the world and going to the war against Iraq and defying the veto that was to be used by France at that time. President Bush made the United Nations one of the organizations he presides. If so, Mr. President; what does the United Nations Secretary General do? Is he there just in an honorary position or to have fun and we do not know about that?

This time, Russia wanted to propose an immediate cease fire. What does the US representative in the United Nations do? Of course, he should practice his capability and hinder peace in case it is for Arabs or Muslims. He has to be a good blocker of moderation and stability in the Middle East, in case he is a Bush representative. He is there to serve Israel. I wonder if he works for America or Israel. Watch out guys because the world is watching you and your cruelty. You cannot defy and keep defying the world all the time. The world is getting sick of your immoral behavior. The world is really tired of you and of the whole Bush administration and their wicked, racist, and ruthless supporters.

Rachel Corrie

I am telling the Americans who support Israel and the racist policy of George W. Bush that they are wrong again. Just go back a few years ago and remember with me the American girl who was ran over by an Israeli bulldozer because she stood their bravely trying to prevent the bulldozer from demolishing a Palestinian house? Don't you think murdering Corrie was a heinous thing to do? If you do not know about that, just please take my advise and make some research about it and you will know who I am talking about. You will also find out that the brave heroine I am telling you about is American from America. She is not an Arab or Palestinian American or a naturalized American citizen. She was not an African American either. By mentioning the color here, I do not mean anything negative. I am trying to tell some of the racist people who do not respect others to watch out because the Israeli murderers are not far from them. Israel has no friend. See what America does to them and how they murder a beautiful young girl like Corrie. Imagine the loss of her parents. Think of her parents' agony and sadness. She was a white American girl from white American parents. I am making everything clear so you do not get mixed up. I am also recalling these facts and incidents so you do not believe I am being prejudiced against Israel or the Israeli people. The Israeli government is the one who makes people hate it, its administration, and the Israeli extremism. I, like all the moderate people in the whole world, have nothing against the other moderate peaceful Jews and Israelis. On the contrary, I respect those moderate people and appreciate their understanding and condemnations of their cruel administration and government.

Rachel Corrie is an American young lady who was murdered by a war criminal, a lousy Israeli soldier who was driving a bulldozer on his way to level a Palestinian house with earth. Corrie was not intimidated by that idiot's threatening. She stood still on the way of the bulldozer. She rejected the Israeli injustice towards Palestinians. Rachel Corrie is a wonderful example of sacrifice, bravery, self-denial, and moderation. She worked for peace. She was not influenced by the disrespectable remarks of Bush and his administrations about Palestinians, Arabs, and Muslims. She used her mind and knew that Bush was a liar like the Israeli leaders. She is the one who deserves to be called a maverick, unlike those who call themselves, their followers, and supporters, mavericks to win the presidential elections. Corrie will always be alive in our minds and hearts. We will never forget you Corrie. We miss you very much. Thank you very much for your great sacrifice with your soul. You did not have to do it but you chose to do it because you are brave. You are much better than the Bush administration and the Israeli officials. You are a lot braver than most of the world leaders who are always silent towards the Israeli crimes and were always mute towards the Bush cruel decisions. Those leaders could not even tell Bush to talk about them with respect. They were his slaves who executed his cruel orders of persecution and injustice.

PEOPLE AND RELIGIONS

I have noticed that many of the American people talk a great deal about religions. Some of them try to convince people their religion is the correct one, and everybody that do not follow them or have another religion will go to hell. A second group follows a certain religion but do not mind others having different religions. A third group follows no religion at all and several people from this group believe that religion is the root and cause of all the evils and wickedness in the world.

Through my own experiences, I have learned that it is not my business to tell people if they should follow a certain religion or not. I honestly did it once during my first year in the states. The response of that friend, whom I advised to follow a religion, was "You can be an excellent missionary!" and that was it. I am neither a missionary nor a preacher. I am just a regular Muslim and Arab person. However, I sometimes talk about religion just in one case. That case is when someone asks and insists that I tell him or her something about a certain issue he or she wants to know about Islam and Muslims. At the same time, I add that there are many resources, sites, and references a person who really wants to know more about Islam can use.

The unfortunate fact is that many of all the above groups still again see Muslims and Arabs as terrorists. You can see that through their own words, sentences, and hints even if they do not see it directly. They mostly like to offend others with their negative remarks. This takes me back to the issue of September 11. I respond again that I had spent three whole years in the United States before September 11 and several Americans always find pleasure making fun of Muslims, Arabs, and Middle Eastern people. In fact, a few months ago, I found that to be an old American habit. Let me tell you how I knew that. One night I was watching the old classic movies channel. I decided to watch it because it was a movie for Stanley Laurel and Oliver Hardy. We love them in Egypt and we used to know them as "the fat and thin" when we were kids. That movie was

CONTINUAL PRETENCES

The Israeli and Bush administrations are making Hamas their continual pretence and excuse. Hamas was not there before 1988. Why was Israel aggressive and used power all the time? They both accused Arafat a few years ago of being the reason of violence and aggression. Where is Arafat now? Is he the reason of this violence? In fact, these continual lies show their cruelness and inhumanity. Look at the war on your TV and computer screens. You see homes and mosques burning and demolishing. Look at the liar Livni who justifies her wickedness by false pretences. Her real goal is well known. It is winning the coming election, especially she had said she will demolish and eradicate Hamas just two days before her war against the poor Palestinians who are dying and running out of fuel, food, and everything.

One of the American writers defended Israel saying a child was killed by Hamas rockets and that is a natural reaction. What about Israelis who killed thousands of children? What about the child, Mohammed El-Dora, the Palestinian boy who was killed intentionally with cold blood by an Israeli soldier in 2000? Why is the Arab blood cheap but the Israelis' is very expensive? Why are there double standard people when it comes to Israel and Arabs? Why cruelty and rudeness? Why are you always against the right in favor of wrong and wicked actions?! The heavy machine guns are striking and killing Palestinians in front of the whole world while this same world is condemning Arabs.

I like to go back to that writer's statement about that rocket that killed an Israeli child? All those children of Palestine who were killed do not count like that Israeli child too! What about the Egyptian officers and soldiers at the borders between Egypt and Israel who were killed during the last few years, in spite of the Egyptian-Israeli peace treaty and agreement. Would Israel have been patient and let it go like that in case those murdered were Israelis killed by Egyptian guns and bullets?! Why do we have to tolerate the Israeli brutality and they do it again and again? Is it enough when they apologize and say it was a mistake?!

Look how Israelis trapped the innocent civilians in their crossfire, the way the trapped Mohammed and his father Jamal El Dora in 2000, killing the little innocent boy and injuring his father. They did not kill his father because their lousy stupid soldier thought he was dead. They have no sense of sensitivity, feelings, or humanity? What do they have? They just have rudeness and boldness. They only know the law of the jungle where the strong attacks the weak. They say they are being attacked. What does an occupation force expect? Flowers, roses, and hugs! No wonder the maverick, Bush, is giving them two weeks to kill, destroy, destruct, and corrupt in Gaza. No wonder that Bush is so happy with his cruelty and wickedness. No wonder you deserve the ugliest pair of shoes Mr. Bush. No wonder....!

The Israeli occupation forces prevented the journalists and photographers from watching and revealing their cruelty. The butchers went on and on butchering Palestinians. The cowards are doing their best to persuade the world that they are moderate. Where is your moderation? Where is your respect of the simplest right for people to live their lives? Where are the other world leaders from this?! They are sitting there either neutral or supporters of Israel. They prove their complicity with the Israeli occupation. They support them indirectly in their murders against the innocent people. They blame their people because they demonstrate against Israel and its cruel actions. They say they did and are still doing whatever they can to stop the Israeli aggression. However, the reality shows the opposite. If they even keep silent, it is very much better for them and their people. Their irresponsible statements cause a lot of wrath and anger. Their blame is just on Hamas as if they were Israelis. For how long are those leaders going to tell us the same thing every time. They do or say nothing but that they are acting wisely and doing whatever they can. What did they do to prevent the wars against Afghanistan and Iraq? What did they do to stop the war against Lebanon? What are they doing to force Israel stop its inhumanity against Palestinians?

Today is January 5, 2009, the 10th day of the severe Israeli war actions continues. Israelis continue targeting civilians. They said they did their best because they care about human life. Tzipi Livni pretends the war actions are going slow because they are worried about their soldiers who can be trapped by Hamas. The killers always find new pretences to stay in the occupied land. They take it for granted that they have every right to act this way against Arabs. They always see themselves to be better than any other race. They show themselves as 'God's chosen people on earth.' For what?! The destruction, the acts of kicking people out of their homes and lands that they have always been famous for, or the continual blame for the rest of the world for the holocaust and the concentration camps?! For how long do you think you can fool the world, like that Jew who said his wife used to go to him every day in his concentration camp to give him an apple. Give us a break and get off our backs. Leave us alone and mind your damn business away from

Palestinians. We can only hope that Obama won't be a second Bush. However, his statements during the presidential transitional periods are no different from Bush. The rumors about him being Muslims are mostly playing an excellent role in his positions and the steps that seem to be taken by him when he takes office. It will be a huge disappointment if he becomes as Bush just to satisfy Israelis. It will be a fatal mistake to dehumanize and look down on Palestinians, like his predecessor, to negate that he is a Muslim. He has the right to correct a wrong piece of information. However, it is neither Bush's nor his right to continue telling us stereotypes about Arabs. Arabs are already fed up with the western world's disrespect, especially from the Bush administration. So, please don't be like Bush who fooled Arabs and made them elect him as president in his first term. Don't be like the racist, reckless people who voted for Bush for a second time. Work for peace. Be your own person and don't be influenced by Bush, Cheney, Rice, and Rumsfeld.

Ehud Barak is telling us today their severe operations will continue until peace and tranquility prevails. Where will peace and tranquility come from?! Your rockets, F16, bulldozers, tanks, ground troops, or extended operations day and night?! Are you fooling us? Why not as long as you have Bush and Rice, who seek durable and sustainable, cease fire? Why not and you have their blessing to go on your holocaust against Arabs? Why not and you have competitions about your Israeli elections? Why not and you have a golden opportunity to kill as many Palestinians as you can? Why not and you are one of the famous butchers and blood lovers? Why not and all your Israeli debates are about how to keep Palestinians live in misery and suffering. Why not and you are trying to kick Palestinians out of the tiny Gaza strip? Is it too much for them to have a small piece of land to live in, which is theirs in the first place, and you occupiers raped and usurped it from them? Of course, you want to extend your Israeli states and take the rest of Arab world and weaken the whole Muslim world. Of course, you have your tactics, which are no secret to anyone. Certainly, you think well and show your greed to the whole world. Look at all the moderate people who are angry with your practices. You are just acting and being dumb, blocking your ears, and turning your faces away from them, you ugly people.

TRUTH IS PAINFUL

Today, I got a feedback from someone who asked to read my book, ***Leave People Alone***. I loaned her a copy. Her feedback was that it is all about me and I am being mistreated…etc. The truth is that people like to see things the way they want and like. The truth is also that the idea of my books is clear but people do not like to hear an honest and straightforward statement. People like hypocrites who deceive them and tell them they are sweet. Several Americans will appreciate my thoughts if I praise them. If I say the truth, I am horrible in their eyes. Therefore, they start talking about the spelling errors, grammar, and accent if it is a verbal conversation or any other thing. How innovative and creative is that! Others took copies of my books, never gave a feedback as they said they were too busy to read. I ask them why they took them in the first place if their invaluable time does not allow them even to read a page. That is really ridiculous and unacceptable. Others knew the books involve some politics and ask for a gift copy and I gave them copies that I already paid for. After that, I got an advice from them not to talk about politics. The question is you know there is politics in them and you said you wanted copies, what does that mean?!

I am really getting sick of people's recklessness. I am fed up with the judgments they make about others. Then, they say it has nothing to do with race, color, religion, or ethnicity. Then what does your racism and hatred have to do with? Do you think because I criticized my boss in the cruise ship who was always making fun of Arabs, I am being bad?! How and what about him?! He is excellent! Maybe as 10 years is more than enough to know and make certain how many Americans, blacks, whites, and native Americas perceive themselves as superiors. Imagine people who start a racist conversation with you and then blame you for not being tolerant. Guess someone starts a dialogue with you by telling you he or she hates your people, guess someone who worships Jesus, who came from Palestine, and then ridicules Arabs and say they are camel jokeys and terrorists. Look at the contradiction. Some of them said they hate Arabs because many Arab women cover their heads. My answer is nuns in America and the rest of the world wear similar head scarf and dress. Why is it acceptable here but not from Arab and Muslim women. As an Egyptian, I have seen Americans who wore bikinis, long and short dresses and skirts, shorts, or whatever they want there. Nobody interferes or tells them what they should or should not do. It is their business and we respect Americans and accept them the way they are there. We do not force them to do something they do not want. Why don't they behave the same way? ***Enough Double Standard!***

Moreover, consider the Arab-Israeli struggle and its phases. The wise people can tell easily that Israel is always the first aggressor. However, Americans like to start other conversations about that struggle showing their prejudice, lack of respect, and hatred towards Arabs. Some like to accuse Arabs of things they have never done or knew the least about. Others, including some of those who criticize my books, do not know anything about the history of that region, how Israel was established in 1948 after raping the Palestinian land, and the long history of the American support to Israel against Arabs. Mommy and daddy had taught them to hate Arabs since their birth. They implanted the hatred of Arabs is in their minds, brains, and hearts. Every day, I can tell why Americans do not respect us. I do not respect the liars who say because of September 11 anymore. Be honest with yourselves and say the truth. Stop fooling yourselves and imagining things you like to see because of your lack of consideration towards Arabs. Give yourselves a second thought about your unjustified racism. I am not saying you have to give up supporting your sweet child, Israel. No, go ahead but at least have some common sense in what you are saying and doing. Just be sure that all people are equal, and you have to admit that, no matter if you have a religion or you are a believer or not. This is your own business. However, your disrespect towards other people is not your business because those others are capable of disrespecting you. Don't act like President Bush who asked, "Why do they hate us?" You took his faulty question and statement for granted as if he never makes mistakes. You increased your already existing hatred and disrespect towards others because of a statement like that. You made Arabs your sole and only enemies. You made Israel your representative and revelation of every wicked thing you do and say. Do you understand what I meant now when I said ***Leave People Alone***? I meant you need to respect people. I also meant those people who said they taught their children to hate Arabs because they attacked America in September 11. Tell me where you got this piece of information from. Where is your proof of what you are saying? Don't tell me Bin Laden's tapes because these kinds of tapes have been faked all over the past century. It is not a big deal to fake tapes, photographs, or videos for anybody. Be honest with yourselves before you leave the main issues and start making fun of people, their accent, language, spelling, or grammar. Also, tell me one more thing. When you go to Egypt and you stop someone to ask about direction or so, don't people help you? It can also be a subject for your fun later to ridicule that person's accent and the way he or she sounds when he speaks English. Fortunately, we don't do that because we respect you as well as every body. We don't discriminate like you. We don't see ourselves as superior to you in our countries. On the contrary, we spare no effort to show you our love, friendship, and appreciation. On the opposite side, you made yourselves our judges and executers. Show some respect to people guys. Don't always find pleasure in dehumanizing us. Don't look at us as if we were inferior to you.

In the last Gaza conflict, many people still say they are with Israel and they have nothing to do with Arabs. My friend Brandon from Indiana called me some months ago to tell me he does not hate Arabs but he supports Israelis when they kill Arabs and kick them out of their houses. Brandon had no reason in his belief. He just grew up that way. I did my part and explained to him what is going on between Israelis and Arabs.

THE COWARDS OF THIS AGE

The coward Israeli leaders bombed the school some Palestinians used as a shelter to hide themselves and their kids from the Israeli fires that surround them everywhere. The UN had informed the Nazi Israelis about the site of the school and ordered them not to target it. As usual, Israelis acted as traitors, hit the school, and killed 40 civilians who do not have the least to do with that issue. The idiots never listen to the sound of wisdom, mercy, or humanity.

A scene in this war, which every decent human being should reject and condemn, is of a mother who called her son who was playing with other children outside their house. The mother asked the boy to fill in a bottle with water from a public fossil outside their house. The boy took the bottle and filled it. When he was entering his house, the house was gone. The Israelis destroyed the house. His mother and the others inside the house were murdered in cold blood. The boy himself, with the other kids, became small pieces by the Israeli artillery. Please tell me if I can keep silent about all this cowardliness, brutality, inhumanity, and indifference about those innocent humans. Is it reasonable to tolerate senseless people such as Bush and Rice in front of all that Israeli violence and aggression?!

President Hugo Chavez of Venezuela acted humanly, wisely, and respectfully towards Muslims, Arabs, and Palestinians. He kicked the Israeli ambassador out of his country. Thank you very much President Chavez. President Chavez always stood strongly in the face of the Israeli aggression towards Palestinians, Arabs, and Muslims. My thanks also extend to Cuba and its former President, Fidel Castro and his brother, the current President Raul Castro. You are really three wonderful presidents and human beings. Thanks for your bravery and support for the conquered Palestinians.

Today is January 7, 2009. The latest news is that Israel hit three schools, not just one. Israel killed more innocent children and women. Israel showed its continual and unprecedented disrespect to the world community. Why not, if the first maverick, George W. Bush and his Secretary of State, Rice are putting all the blame on Hamas? Why not when Bush and Rice are acting like Mommy and Daddy for the sweet child, Israel?! Why not and the rest of the world is doing nothing but condemning, rejecting, consulting?

The lovely Israel finally gave Gazans a truce for a whole three hours. See how nice, three whole long complete hours and then started bombing and destructing again. A TV announcer was wishing that the Palestinian civilians were all back to their homes because the bombing and killing began again. What is the benefit my dear if Israel targets the homes of innocent people?! Didn't Israel demolish the three schools used as shelters that were identified by the UN and targeted them? Then, we say Israel committed a new massacre. Be honest guys. Don't be so nice and say it is one massacre. It is three schools' massacres.

We as Arabs know and understand that it is not a mistake that Israelis target children as Israel always says and pretends after incidents like that, which she does purposely all the time. We are proud that Israel is scared of those little children. We know that Israel kills and destroys them before they grow up and seek revenge as Israel believes, like us, that Israelis will be kicked out of the Palestinian and Arab lands by children. No matter what Israelis do by challenging us, they are not and cannot challenge God. During the last 20 years, Israel's main concern was fighting Palestinians and promoting its war machine to eradicate them. Israel cannot use her weapons against another weapon that God has donated the Palestinians, which is the fertility weapon. Studies proved that Palestinians multiply more than Israelis, at least twice the number of Israelis' multiplying. The highest percentage of the world fertility is in Palestinians.

Anyway, Israel has always to be excused for its own wickedness and cruelty. Israel was sweet enough to give three hours truce, not a day or two. No, three whole damn hours. Thanks kind-hearted Israel. Thanks our spoilt baby. Go ahead, kill, destroy, destruct, demolish, amputate, and burn. Then, get paid as usual for your good deeds. We are in the Mavericks' age and you are one of those mavericks, whom nobody can stop.

SEAN HANITY

Fox News' Sean Hanity is one of the new mavericks of this age. This maverick reached the climax after September 11, 2001 when he started giving and developing his brilliant and unprecedented thoughts. His racism and hatred towards all Muslims and Arabs have been always obvious. His clear double standard is also no secret. That is why he became very famous as everyone knows how Sean Hanity is. Why not, otherwise how come he is a magnificent maverick?

Anyone who watches Fox News could tell how Hanity misrepresent people and interpret everything the way he wants. Hanity has his own talented revelations, which he pours in his audience minds. He never tries to be objective. Remember with me how Hanity used to talk about President Obama and Vice President Joe Biden. Look how Hanity is always a wonderful representation for every Republican figure, action, and decision. See how different Hanity is when it comes to Democrats. Hanity then talks about racism, disrespect, and arrogance.

Please let someone else talk about those issues, dear Hanity. You are a real misrepresentation for any moderate person, view, or idea. You are the racism itself. In fact, you are the master of racism and hatred. You always tell your guests who oppose you that they should be ashamed of themselves and you know nothing about shame, shame on you, Hanity. You are the one who should be ashamed of himself but I doubt it. It seems you never admitted you were wrong like President Bush, Vice President Dick Cheney, and their Secretary of State, Condoleezza Rice.

Hanity, you are blaming Palestinians of being racist because they are demonstrating against the Israelis' war actions in Gaza. You see Palestinians as racist because some of them raised signs telling Israelis, "Go back to the oven." Is this racist but the killing of innocent Palestinians and disproportion Israel uses in its war, as it's always her habit, with Palestinians is not? Stop your media war against Islam, Muslims, and Arabs. Before you criticize people, go ahead and get over your obvious ignorance and arrogance. Read some history. Go back and see how Israel was established and how Israelis kicked Palestinians out of their homeland. Learn how to respect others. You should be taught some lessons about ethics and manners. People like you, Hanity, are a bad representation for America. People who know nothing about respect and consideration for others' feelings, culture, religion, and traditions are worth contempt, and you are one of those people. It is unfortunate for one of the biggest and most famous news channels to have a host like you.

However, I have all the respect and appreciation for your co-host Alan. Alan is a very respectable announcer who gives a chance to his guests to say whatever they feel. He does not always interrupt them like you. He does not applaud and praise them just because they are from the Republican Party or supporters of Republicans like you. Thanks Alan for not being like your friend. I hope he learns to respect people the way you respect them. I wish he grows up and admits he can be wrong sometimes, like any human being. When Hanity does that, we can call him a real maverick then. When he stops accusing honest people of being arrogant and reckless, he will prove he learned a good lesson. He should know how to judge himself before he judges other people. Hanity is always upset when someone criticizes him. Those people are saying nothing but the truth. How about you who likes to degrade people all the time? Why don't you think about their feelings the way you think about yours?!

It seems Hanity likes to be controversial just for the sake of controversy, which is fine, but try to have your arguments built on facts. You cannot argue with people about a subject you do not know the least about. Get yourself some culture then go ahead and educate people as you always try to do. You have to educate yourself first about every subject you talk about. You do not have one single idea about the nature of the Arab-Israeli conflict. I am an Egyptian who studied and experienced it. I remember the days of my childhood when we were living in horror because of Israel. I never forgot the sound of the danger sirens and how we used to run and hide whenever we heard it any time we are out, day and night. I still recall the sound of the volunteers' whistles who yelled at us to turn the lights off because of the continual Israeli incursions. I still remember my friends, classmates, and neighbors who were evacuated from the Suez Canal states; Port Said, Suez, and Ismailia because of the total and fatal destruction of their homes. Can you imagine all these three states were completely evacuated? You could see nothing but destruction and death.

Israel also occupied the Egyptian peninsula of Sinai in 1967. When it left Sinai, Israel could not do it without doing a lot of destruction such as exploding the water wells, demolishing the magnificent buildings, and destroying lots of trees and plants. Israel acted as if how come I get out of Sinai and leave everything the same way, forgetting that Sinai is Egyptian and not Israeli in the first place. This is how Israel also acted when it evacuated Gaza, ***that false evacuation,*** during Ariel Sharon's era. It destroyed all the houses Israelis had to evacuate. It looks like they show and stress their hatred for Palestinian, whom they raped their lands, killed their relatives, and imprisoned their brothers, sister, sons, and daughters without a reason. After all that, Israelis pretend they are the chosen people of God on earth. What for? Why do you think so highly of yourselves? If you really see yourselves this way, act as decent human beings so people can see and agree that you are correct. Unfortunately, all your actions show the opposite. You did nothing to make you the chosen people. The ways you always act explain that you are the hated and aggressive people. Your destruction of mosques and churches is not an act of God's favorite people. It is the behavior of damned and cursed race who despise every other race, culture, and religion. The superiority you give yourselves is false. Your superiority is actually nothing but inferiority. The excuses you have always found to attack Arabs are false. The support of George W. Bush is not eternal. Your maverick's era is coming to an end or already ended. As your maverick's end, you are also coming to an end. This is always the end of injustice and cruelty. None of the current Israeli leaders is a man or woman of his or her word. How could they be and they never apply their treaties or charters? They step on everything and everyone to achieve their greedy colonization goals. Why not if they bomb Iraq and Syria's nuclear reactors and get away with their actions? Why not and their racist supporters always have their ready-made accusations of terrorism towards Arabs? Why not and several extremists in the world show Israelis their sympathy stressed with a great deal of anger towards Muslims and Arabs? Why not and they have people like Sean Hanity who sees Palestinians' demonstrations against aggression as racism and anti-Semitic? Why not and ignorant people all over the world are cheering for Israel? They just do that because they were not taught to respect others.

HINDERING AIDS

The Israeli army and officials targeted the aids that were sent to Gaza for the innocent civilian Palestinians. The Israeli cowards murdered a UN truck driver. Again, this shows the continual contempt of the innocent souls and lives. It is disrespect towards the UN, its employees, and leadership. It is also lack of consideration of the world's feelings. It does not show the least sign of concern about anyone or anything. Israel always acts as if it were a country above any international regulations or laws. Israel should not be an exception that always gets away with whatever it does under the pretence that "Israel has the right to defend itself." I repeat again that Bush and Rice used that opinion and sentence frequently until we learned it by heart. I see it this way: When you have a spoilt child whom you give anything he or she asks for and you keep doing that all the time, that child will rebel against you, if you once refused to satisfy his or her needs. Several world leaders such as Bush and Blair acted this way and are still proud of themselves for their racism and cruelty. How come they can tell Israel to stop now? Why shouldn't Israel put her tongue out to them and the rest of the world now? Do you see how the Supreme Israeli state acts? However, I am one of the people who refuse that supremacy of Israel. I am not a world leader. I am a regular person who feels the sufferings of other people. I am a person who refuses the Israeli lies when it shows false pictures of Palestinians dancing after September 11 to make the whole world hate them and say they deserve what the cruel Israeli state and government do to them. I still remember how Israel used 9/11 to kill more Palestinians. The whole world was busy with 9/11 and that was a golden opportunity for Israel. Arafat, the one you always disrespected and perceived to the whole world as a terrorist, donated his blood to the 9/11 victims and told his people to act the same way. The double standard Bush and his officials did not appreciate that for him. None of the Israeli maverick leaders acted the same way. They just used 9/11 as one more new weapon towards Palestinians, Arabs, and Muslims. Bush was a great help as he spared no effort to destroy

Afghanistan and Iraq, acting as a server for the Israeli privileges in the Middle East and the whole Muslim world. The American maverick helped the Israeli mavericks to weaken the Middle East and consume its sources, burn its oil wells, and destroy its economy.

Although I do not have the least idea how Obama's policy towards Israel and the Middle East will be, I am glad McCain was not elected. It is a blessing as the world had enough mavericks that are fond of destroying and increasing its misery as long as such misery does not reach them. This is the selfishness of colonialism and occupation. However, the simplest international laws say that the occupation forces have to protect the occupied civilian people. Israel never does that. Israel always kills innocent Palestinians. Then, Israel pretends it's Hamas that makes civilians human shields. Again, I will prove to you that the Israeli officials are liars because Hamas was not there before 1988. Hamas is a fairly new group. Before Hamas was established, Israel killed the innocent people. Hamas is just a good excuse for Israel at this time as Israel always has its well-decorated excuses. The moderate world sees the Israeli lies while Bush is still blessing the killing of the innocent Palestinian women, children, and elderly people. However, we cannot deny how Bush is very considerate and kind-hearted. The man and his family had an official White House statement mourning the death of his daughters' cat. That is really a nice thing to do and I am not sarcastic here. But the man who mourns a cat should feel sorry for the children and women who were bombed in the schools of the United Nations that were used as shelters for the innocent civilian Palestinians. The man who mourns a cat should not always give the Israelis the green light to murder Palestinians. Israel always acts as it is going on a pleasing hunting trip. Israel hunts people, not deer. Israel aims its dangerous modern arms towards armless people.

Israel is also the one who killed the Palestinians in the summer of 1982 in the refugees' camps of Sabra and Shatila in Lebanon. The leader of those dirty unethical killing operations was Ariel Sharon, who is seen as a man of peace by George W. Bush. Look how a dirty blooded handed person like Sharon is a man of peace and Arafat is a terrorist. How can Arafat who was defending Palestine and its freedom be seen as a terrorist and the real terrorist is appreciated for his wicked behavior! What a nice world we live in!

For your information, if you do not know, Sharon and his soldiers killed every single creature they could see then. They refused to leave horses and dogs alive and executed them with their guns and bullets. Sharon is one of the prominent leaders in the schools of violence who are imitated by Ehud Barak, Ehud Olmert, and Tzipni Livni. It is not strange after all that to find a song that says, "I love Amre Mousa and hate Israel." That is very natural as Amre Mousa is a man of peace. He is the Arab league Secretary General and was the Egyptian Foreign Minister before that. It is also clear to the moderate world that people love peacemakers and hate aggressor people and nations. Israel has been an aggressor nation since its establishment in 1948. Consider the difference between Amre Mousa, the popular Egyptian man and the lousy Israeli officials. You will see a great difference. It is the difference between respect and disrespect, love and hatred, peace and war, friendship and aggression, and nobility and vulgarity.

THE SECURITY COUNCIL AND THE CEASE FIRE

Tonight is the eighth of January, 2009. The UN Security Council had a meeting to put an end to the war between Israel and Hamas. To be more precise and exact, the real aim is to stop the Israeli inhuman crimes towards Palestinians. Rice, representing the US abstained, while 14 countries agreed to the immediate cease fire. Rice said nothing important, just going around the same issue again and again of durable and sustainable cease fire. She chose to end her era with the Bush administration with racism towards Muslims and Arabs as it has always been their hobby and habit. CNN's Richard Roth and Christian Amanpour were more than excellent covering the incident from New York and Jerusalem. Their political and broadcasting experience were clear in discussing Rice's position and the end of her era with that unjustified abstained vote. However, we thank you Rice for not using the veto against the helpless Palestinians. It is really the age of power and aggression. This is why the powerful America, represented by you and George W. Bush, is always helping, protecting, and supporting the mighty Israel towards every Palestinian, Arab, and Muslim concern.

Israel cries for a single soldier whom she says Hamas is keeping as a captive. How about all the Palestinian women, men, and children who are imprisoned in the Israeli jails? Are these thousands worthless and one Israeli soldier is worth all that killing and destruction?! ***Stop the Double Standard***.

THE CONTINUAL ISRAELI LIES AND
THE WORLD'S GREAT SUPPORT

Today is the 9th of January, 2009. Israel announced that it did not target the UN truck and its driver of the human aid support to the civilian people of Gaza. Israel did not even say it was a mistake, a "friendly fire," or whatsoever of the meaningless phrases of the cruel, ugly, and inhuman wars of our time. Israel pretends it's not her that hindered the UN effort. Israel is still trying to deceive us. Israel fooled the world for several decades using what she calls holocaust and concentration camps. The butchers of our age are denying their lousy crimes. Why do you deny it? Do you think it will make a difference? Probably, but not for us, your denial might make a difference for Bush, Cheney, and Rice.

The American double standard and prejudice against Muslims and Arabs continue. Moreover, it is reaching its climax. Recall with me the California African American who was held by three police officers then shot and killed by one of them. Did you see the anger, the demonstration, and the burning and damaging of the police car? I totally agree that what happened by that policeman is a heinous crime and should not just go like that. He should pay for his unjustified crime, like any killer or criminal. You are right that criminals do not deserve our sympathy, love, or support. Consider with me how this city rose up against that policeman and other innocent policemen who have nothing to do with that murder. Remember how that lady came on the TV screen telling us that they (the police) are terrifying them and therefore they have to be terrified and live in horror like them. Remember the man who was shouting in the microphone saying, "We need justice right now."

Remember all that with me. Think very well about it and you will understand my point then. The point is what happened to that murdered man is terrorism. You responded to such terrorism and did things that should have never happened such as burning, destroying, and blaming the whole police community. What about the poor, helpless Palestinians who experience the Israeli state terrorism every single day?! What in the world should they do when they get kicked out of their houses and have the Israelis demolish them? In fact, this happens if they are lucky and Israel allows them out. Several times Israel demolished innocent people's houses when they are sleeping, eating, studying, watching TV, or just sitting in their homes having a family friendly conversation. So please, stop the double standard and give Palestinians the rights you give to yourselves. Stop looking down on others and always remember that "all men are created equal." I am not better than you and you are not better than me because you are American and I am not.

Last week, during this Israeli ethnic war against Gaza, I was watching CNN. I watched that program for the announcer who I can remember his name as Rick. I do not really recall the full name but he is a real good and talented announcer. I also know he is bilingual as he speaks English and Spanish fluently. I remember that day because he had his son whom I think have the same name, Rick on his program. Before that, Rick was talking about the Hamas leader who was the killed when Israel bombed and demolished his house with their F16s. Rick first said, "When you know what happened you feel angry then you hear what the guy said, you do not know…" Please Rick! Let me explain something and be patient with me, you and all my dear readers of course. This guy and others did not start like that. They were living in peace with their families but Israel do not let them live in peace. Israel denies them the simplest right anyone can have, which is the right of a decent life. It is not just the right of a decent life, but the right to have even the dirtiest and most miserable kind of life, Rick. Please recall what happened by Israel in 2000 when it killed too many Palestinians. Remember with me that child, Mohammed El-Dora who was killed by an Israeli soldier with his automatic gun, and his father who was injured dangerously then just because they were walking in the street.

What in the world is that kind of life, Rick? Rick! I also blame you for one more sentence you said to your producer or photographer then which was, "Get rid of him." That was when you were showing a previous statement for that Hamas leader before his murder. You won't talk about an Israeli this way, Rick. Please remember that Palestinians are human beings too like Americans and Israelis and have to be respected, appreciated, or at least left alone. Moreover, if you and several Americas were going to support the killing of that Hamas leader, why do you still support the killing of all his four wives and children with him? Why is it alright for Israel to demolish people's houses? Is it going to build them other houses if they lived? It is very clear that Israel is trying to have Palestinians kicked out of Gaza and all the parts of Palestine and Israel. Israel wanted all those Palestinians left there to flee their homes and country. Then, they go and seek political refugee anywhere else in the world. We all understand that. That is why Hamas is responding to all the unjustified Israeli wars, incursions, and destructions.

I mentioned earlier how Israel thinks and acts. Israel is a state that does not respect its treaties and agreements. Every time before any due date to execute a treaty and surrender from any land it occupies, Israel starts some factions by killing innocent people, pretending they are terrorists or support terrorism. In turn, some Palestinians retaliate. Such retaliation and *response* to the Israeli massacres and terrorism is always seen and described by our unfair world as terrorism. Look how Israel acts and stop the double standard. ***STOP THE DOUBLE STANDARD.***

Today, a Hamas leader assured that they want peace but Israel does not give them that chance. The Hamas leader also wondered how they could be peaceful while Israel is bombing them from the air, the land, and the sea. We have to be reasonable before making ourselves judges against Palestinians. We have to put ourselves in their position before saying they are terrorists and aggressors.

The fact is that Israel thinks it can wipe off Palestinians from the surface of the earth. Israel believes she can do that and then eventually wipe off all the Arabs and then all the Muslims all over the world. Israel also thinks she can do every damn thing she wants. She found great support from America and England who planted her in Palestine in 1948. Therefore, it is more than alright to do and act the same way in order to invade more countries and achieve its great dream of the Greater Israel. Israel took it for granted then that she can get away with anything. No, My dear Israel, no, and million no. You cannot always get away with whatever you want to do. No, my dear spoilt child. You should know your limits and stop exceeding them. Stop crossing all the red lines, defying the moderate world community, and challenging all the peaceful people all over the world. You did more than enough.

What a good joke it is when the Israeli leaders do the same thing over and over again under the false pretence of defending themselves! Changing their meetings for meetings to achieve peace agreements into security meeting became their model and standard of dealing with Palestinians. Sharon was one of the mavericks who invented, promoted, and developed that method. Viva Sharon, you and those who are following your steps.

DEFYING HUMAN RIGHTS

The Israeli leaders are defying everyone, everything, and every simple human law and convention. Where are the human rights' organizations from what is happening in Gaza? How can those leaders go away with their murders and crimes? How can they demolish people's homes on their heads like that and level them with the ground? In what law or constitution is that, the law of Bush, Rice, Livni, and Olmert? How in the world are we silent like that? What negotiations are these people talking about? What the hell is this negotiating? We have been negotiating with Israel for decades and what did we get from such negotiations? Are we lying to ourselves or just do that to pretend we spared no effort to help Gaza and Palestine? What are we doing? We are insulting and humiliating ourselves by negotiating with Israel who knows nothing but killing and destructing. We have stretched our hands to Israel very welcomingly. What was the result? Israel killed our soldiers on the borders and stabbed us in the back multiple times. How can we then listen to Israel and invite their leaders to negotiate with us on our land? Israel does not pay us the least attention or respect and we pay her a great deal of attention. We show her respect and appreciation that she does not deserve at all. Israeli leaders are worth nothing but our contempt and hatred. The haters and murderers should be avoided, at least, if we can do nothing to stop their bullies and butchers.

Now it is the first month for President Obama's first term and Israel started seizing more Palestinian lands to expand her settlements and allow more Israeli settlers to move to the Palestinian territories. What is the result of that? More defying to the world community and a great deal more factions between Israelis and Palestinians will occur. If an Israeli is injured or killed, he or she will be a victim of terrorism and terrorists. If the same happens with a Palestinian, it will be the same issue of "Israel has the right to defend itself."   Olmert, the Israeli prime minister is pretending he is achieving a part of a peace agreement with Palestinians, which gives him the right of constructing more houses in the West Bank. Here we go. The lies continue and spread again. Olmert adds he has the right to widen the Israeli settlements. Olmert gives himself such rights, tells people Palestinians are willing to do that, and what do you think to happen next? Can we blame Palestinians when they object and defend their lands?!

Moreover, look at one of the expected persons to take office as the new Israeli prime minister. It is Benjamin Netanyahu who supports increasing and enlarging the Israeli settlements. Netanyahu also rejects peace talks or negotiations with Palestinians, pretending it is a waste of time. Isn't that the same line of Bush and Sharon? It is because the maverick Netanyahu is following the same steps and that is nothing new for him.

THE REQUIRED SOLIDARITY

I
f we cannot stop the Israeli Barbaric invasion on Gaza by force, all of us need to do something to help. All what we can do is important. We do not want to leave Israel corrupt on earth any way she wants. Israel should not be an exception. Israel does not have the right to do that to us. Israel is a real obvious gang that practices and spreads terrorism directly and indirectly. The direct terrorism starts from its own leaders while the indirect starts and comes as a reaction to its unjustified strikes, murders, crimes, and aggressions. The evil country of Israel believes she can have everyone submit and surrender to its occupational needs. If George W. Bush gives them that right of injustices and discrimination, it is his business. It is Bush's business now to mind his own business as he is not a president anymore. He imposed his prejudice, racism, and contempt against the whole world for eight whole years. We are fed up with him, his practices, and crazy statements. He applauded for every terrorist act against Arabs and saluted it. He worked all his era as an Israeli agent who is stationed in the US. Bravo Bush! You deserve a new prize they should invent and make you the first receiver of it. It is the International Prize for Racism, Murders, and Destruction. You said you will make the world a safer place but you made it a jungle. You increased terrorism and terrorists. Gaza's war is the most recent example of terrorism you started, supported, and embraced. There is no wonder when a student in a high school in Dear Born once wore a shirt has your picture and under it had the words 'International Terrorist' The school officials then made it a big deal and ordered the student to take that shirt off and I don't know why they did that. Couldn't they see then the destruction you caused in Afghanistan and Iraq? Didn't they see the pictures of the Guantanamo Bay Prisoners? Couldn't they tell that you are really an international terrorist who practiced terrorism under a high level through your scrutiny of all the people's phones, computers, and communications? Couldn't they see how you talked about other people with recklessness, indifference, and disrespect? How can you give yourself the

right to invade people's privacy like that under the pretence of the patriot act and protection of America?

You made several people lose their confidence and trust in the government. Many people who supported you turned against you later after they discovered the lies. Some of your administration's officials revealed your lies. You left no room for confidence or trust.

BRACE FOR WAR ESCALATION

After more than two weeks of its unjustified war, Israel drops more leaflets over Gaza. What in the world do you want the people to do? You are killing them and insist on their death anyway through your bombs, hunger, jails, or whatsoever. You are inventors of all the lousy, stupid, and ugly methods in your wars and aggressions against Muslims and Arabs. You are the real reckless Nazis. Your ugly leaders have to be tried for all the crimes they do and commit every single day.

What is the benefit of those leaflets you merciless people if you do not offer those people another place to live in? What the hell do you think you're doing? Get off our back stupid idiots, shame on you and those who support you. Shame also on the helpless world, which just rejects, condemns, and feels sorry for the victims. Aren't there international forces to stand against Israel? Why were those forces just used against Iraq, fair rulers, leaders, and mavericks? Because Iraq is a Muslim and Arab country?! It does not mean anything else. This proves every single day that you are launching an extended violent war against Islam. Unfortunately, several Muslim leaders are helping you achieving your dirty goals. That is why there is no wonder that their people are demonstrating against them and expressing their feelings of hatred and disgust towards those traitors who brought us nothing but shame and misery, shame on you miserable leaders. You disgraced us either with your support to Bush or silence to Israel's continual massacres in Gaza and all over Palestine, the occupied Palestine, which they colonized in 1948 and named Israel.

Had they passed with their lousy occupation, raped the land, and settled there despite the will of all Muslims and Arabs, they should have respected the Palestinians and let them live a decent life in their own *Home*. They did not; they never did, and will never do. They are just fooling us and we are fools to trust them. How can we trust people who always proved to be traitors? How do we allow ourselves to fall in their traps all the time? What in the world makes us keep listening to people who do not give a damn about us? Why do we give them the impression that our blood is cheap and theirs is invaluable? We prove that we never learn from the lessons of the past. We see them disrespect us at the universal, political, psychological, sociological, societal, and personal levels. Then, we do not move a thumb to object. It is exactly like when two school kids have a fight. The strong one with bigger body and stronger muscles beats the weak one and defeats him. That is how Israel acts. Israel displays her power in arms and guns, bullies her Arab neighbors, and more important and significant, bullies their hosts, the Palestinians, who are the natives of what they called Israel in 1948.

I wonder if someone can deny that the Israeli leaders are bullies except for Bush and his administration. It is true that we blame the rest of the world for doing nothing to prevent such barbarism. However, the other world with its leaders was not racist, mean, and irresponsible like Bush, Rice, and the Bush supporters and administration. Today, two days after the Security Council resolution for the immediate cease fire, Israel killed 30 persons who have nothing to do with Hamas. We let it go as usual. I need some wise person to tell and explain to me what is the benefit of the United Nations resolutions if they cannot be respected and implemented? Is it just a waste of time, money, paper, and ink? Do all these UN representatives, ministers, and delegators just meet in New York for fun? Ok! Alright! Someone will say the UN and its Security Council did what they can. No, they did not. What did they do when they were against Bush's reckless war against Iraq? Could they prevent him? Is it a rule that Bush and Israel are untouchable? Nobody can hinder them back when they are wrong! I believe the UN Secretary General and the Security Council President should have the power to order them to surrender and submit to the will of the world community. Otherwise, there is no need or use for the UN, and I mean it. Neither Bush nor Israel is the God of the Universe. I say that because they really act as if they were the Lords of our World. They act like the Pharaoh when he said, "I am your supreme God." They do not see themselves as regular people like us. Who distinguished these people, the fake votes, the military power, and operations?! It is not brave to fight someone who is weaker than me. It is a cowardly act. Look at the disproportion of the war against Iraq. It is not surprising when Iraqi and Palestinian officials said in both times about Iraq and Gaza that is "The Law of the Jungle." We live in a jungle ruled by George W. Bush and Israel. Look at both wars. Doesn't it look like a jungle in which the lion is fighting a rabbit or a mouse?! Consider the cowardly acts of Israel, which responds to some children who defend themselves with rocks by tanks and helicopters. Israel which uses all her arsenal towards poor and helpless people says it defends itself. If you defend yourself, Israel, you should defend it against yourself, your greed, your dream of expanding yourself by raping people's land. Look at the history of those Palestinians you disrespect. Consider how many years of civilization they have and how old you are. You are a bastard child, and here, I am addressing Israel and not Judaism. As a Muslim, I believe in Judaism. Is it an act of manhood or humanity to target the ambulance that moves the people you injured and amputated to hospitals? It is a cowardly act, like you cowards. Is it reasonable to bomb the trucks that carry food and aids to those helpless people? Is it alright when you kill infants who are still in the pumpers?

You get angry when actors all over the world show your inhumanity in their plays, TV shows, and movies. Get angrier because they will show your real face, you double faced state. You think you are above any criticism or rejection of your wickedness. You deny you are wicked. Wickedness can be ashamed of you because you exceeded and excelled it. If you hold any responsibility and respect towards the rest of the world, you should have done your best to avoid targeting civilians. You should have never demolished one house or destroyed the crops of Palestinians. You should have never prevented workers to cross your mean checkpoints to go to their jobs and works. You leave them no chance to like, appreciate, or welcome your presence. You are unwelcomed guests who imposed themselves on the homeowners by force and through your bullies. You do not know how to respect yourselves so others can respect you. You are hypocrites who say something to the international community and always do the opposite. You always like to trap Palestinians by starting killing them. When they respond or retaliate, you get your real golden chance to kill the largest number you can. Tell me again, why did you demolish the houses in Gaza after what you called your surrender from it? Were they mobile homes you can move? No, they were not. If they were, who could blame you? Nobody but that is the way you are, fond of destruction, corruption, and lousiness, you lousy losers. You said you made a great sacrifice then by surrendering from Gaza. It is not yours robbers and usurpers. Gaza is Palestinian, not Israeli and it will never be an Israeli land. Gaza is a Palestinian and Arab land owned by the Palestinian people, Muslims and Christians.

I also have a question and an addition here to all the religious people who follow Jesus. I am a Muslim who believes in Jesus. Our belief in Jesus is different from yours as many of you say he is the Savior and the God. However, we both believe in Jesus and our differences should not weaken us. As long as we can respect one another, that is what matters. Another issue about religion, who is right, and who is wrong is not ours. That is God's business. As we both believe in God, we should not argue about that.

My point here is after spending years in America is why many Americas, including those who follow Jesus Christ, do not respect the Arab people. I always say it that Jesus is from Palestine. He is from that area you look down on its people. There is no reason for you to be prejudiced and haters of Arabs. Arabs did not hurt you. Otherwise, if it is just a way you are brought up to hate Arabs for no reason or just for the sake of hatred, you are "crusaders" like George W. Bush. Arabs respect and like you. Have respect for them and show them appreciation even once.

Israel pretends that the United Nations' resolution is "unworkable." How in the world you made it unworkable? What the hell you want?! Palestine is an Arab and Palestinians are not giving it up. It is their land, not yours. They are the ones who defend themselves. They are also the ones who have the upper hand and who should say what is workable and what is not. Your fires are everywhere burning and choking people with your smoke. Isn't this a holocaust? Are you human beings? Is it possible to have 40 air raids on Gaza the second day after issuing the Security Council Resolution? How cowards you are!

Moreover, Livni announced that Israel is the only one who can decide when to cease fire, continuing putting her tongue out to everyone and every convention. Israel continues the indifference. Israel thinks it can have peace, stability, and cease fire from the other side. However, it does not want to cease fire from her side. How can peace be achieved then? The Israeli people who say that they love others, respect them, and want them to live in peace show their daily hatred towards Palestinians, Arabs, and Muslims. The ridiculous nature of our world is to listen to the Israeli and reject the Arab view.

Malcolm X (Al-Hajj Malik El-Shabazz)

One of the double standard American issues that I just knew last night is the complete ignorance of Mr. Malcolm X (Al-Hajj Malik El-Shabazz). I just learned about him from my dear friend Sonya McIntyre Handy. The ignorance to Hajj Malik is due to the fact that he was Muslim. He does not get even 1% of what Dr. Martin Luther king gets. The media does not even talk about him in his birthday or day of assassination. Why the double standard if you really do not discriminate because of color or religion? It does not make any sense. I do not believe that you are really moderate or neutral. I do not deny that Dr. King played a great role in the modern history of America and the liberation of the Blacks in America. However, Hajj Malik played an important role too. He invited people to respect each other. Why giving all the attention to Dr. King and ignoring an important figure in the history of America like Malcolm X?!

According to Sonya McIntyre-Handy, US Federal Precedent Law Writer (McIntyre-Handy v Commonwealth of Virginia 1997) Eastern District Federal Court said:

Malcolm X's current non-recognition of his participation by the news media, which was enormous during the civil rights movement in the 1960s is what I feel, is particularly because of him being non-Christian. History was so illustrative during the 1960's era of his participation and empowering black minorities to self-respect, thus, giving Blacks a sense of identity, heritage, and empowerment. For him to be reduced is to negate the very history in facts that led to the current changes that we all have benefitted from. Martin Luther King's contribution has been so illustriously demonstrated in our current celebration because I feel he is a Christian, which makes our very history discriminatory. Both men contributed to peace for minorities. They may have chosen different path with the same ends. (2009).

Malcolm X saw the white man as his enemy but he said some of them are not the Blacks' enemy. Malcolm X said that prior to his pilgrimage to Makkah. He insisted that the American

Blacks are nothing but second class citizens and former slaves. He added if you like it or not, it is the truth. Malcolm saw that if America has the right to draft people to defend her abroad, people there has the right to defend themselves (Malcolm X, 1963). Malcolm explained that Islam is his religion and his religion is his personal business. He invited people to keep their religions in their homes and not to make religions a means of disputes and differences. He also believed that it is unfair when Whites take charge of everything. He said that the man who controls is the one who does not look like what Blacks do. Blacks then find themselves trapped. The black man had to know and understand the importance of starting business. This eliminates the Blacks' relying on others for their jobs. Malcolm assured the necessity of keeping the person's religion between him or her and God, whether a Christian or Muslim. He complained about the Blacks' suffering from political oppression and economic crises. He invited people "to stop singing and start swinging" (Malcolm X, 1964).

Malcolm X (1964) insisted that the government then had failed the Blacks. This is the way I see the damage that happened in the period between 2000 to the beginning of 2009 because of George W. Bush and his cruel and reckless administration. Malcolm X stressed the importance of Nationalism. I agree with him and with all what he had mentioned. The United States needs to learn from the lessons of the past, stress, and enhance the importance of Nationalism but not by following the way of George W. Bush and his crusades. The crusader, Bush, already damaged the picture of America nationally and internationally. He did not nationalize and unite. Bush separated, segregated, and aggressed. He killed innocent people by his lies. After that, he did not want the Iraqi journalist to throw his shoes at him. Malcolm X (1964) also addressed an important fact, which we still see today. Malcolm X explained how politicians lie during their election campaign and give people false promises. Then, they forget about all what they had said and promised. He also added that they do not live the American dream but the American nightmare. That is what George W. Bush had done. He made us live a nightmare. He encouraged racist people to accuse Arabs and Muslims of terrorism. He made any fantasizing idiot able to put an Arab or a Muslim in jail. He terrorized people with Guantanamo Bay, the way he allowed corruption, injustice, and inhumanity in Abu Gharib, the Iraqi notorious prison. The way Malcolm X talked about Blacks in the 1960s is exactly the way I see Bush and his administration dealt with the Arab and Muslim Worlds nowadays. Malcolm X accused the president and the government then of being segregators. That is the way Bush segregated America and made a huge barrier between America and the moderate world. Unfortunately, Bush found some puppet rulers such as Tony Blair, the former British Prime Minister. No wonder that I met some British citizens who said they could not stand Tony Blair. Who can stand Bush or Blair unless he or she is a racist, segregator, and hater? George W. Bush is exactly like the description of Malcolm X about the aggressor whose brain and power are in bullets, helicopters, and guns. Like what Malcolm

X said, "The government had failed us." I say the same about Bush and his administration who were "involved in a conspiracy" to violate our rights. Bush and his administrators are violators who violated our human rights and should be brought to justice. Bush should be tried as a war criminal. He needs to pay for his cruelty although he is not going to bring an innocent soul back to life. He is not going to heal the injured, amputated, and disfigured persons. Malcolm X said that unity is the sole way to achieve goals and have victory. Freedom does not come with silence but through persistence and continual trials.

AMERICA AND GAZA

Several Americans have been talking about Arabs' leaving America alone and mind their own business. How can this happen if America is the one who supports Israelis with the modern arsenals and weapons? How can it happen if America never shows neutrality when it comes to Israel and Arabs?! How can it occur? How can Arabs do that if America always says that terrorism is Arab and Muslim?! When America shows some respect to Arabs, Arabs can stop thinking that America is always against them, their unity, and stability.

Israel continues targeting the human aids, the ambulances, and all the kind of support to the Palestinians and America keeps saying and announcing its proverb, which you must have learned with me now by heart, from the continual repetition here, in the media, and the newspapers that "Israel has the right to defend itself." Moreover, Israel uses weapons that are internationally forbidden, which burn the body, amputates, cut the heads, and even can break the body into small pieces or into two halves. Then, we still hear the common saying of Israel's self-defense. Which self-defense is that one that responds with these dangerous forbidden weapons that responds to primitive rockets and even rocks thrown by the little kids?! Where is the moderate world? Where are the honest people who can fear nobody or nothing to tell the truth, and not lie to us like the Israeli leaders and George W. Bush?! Can that happen one day? Hopefully it happens in our lifetime.

Israel acts as if it tries its military training and tests these weapons on the women and children. Israel made the Palestinians its target whom she can shot and kill whenever she wants. That was their lousy mean way in every single piece of land their feet touched. A trusted Lebanese friend once told me that he had an Israeli colleague in the institute he used to study at in Detroit. That Israeli told him that they used to go to Lebanon during that miserable era of the Israeli occupation to Lebanon, aim at the Lebanese people, and shot them because they were on a trip to practice hunting.

Whatever you do Israel, the rocks of the young Palestinian children is stronger and more effective than your war machine, guns, and F16s. Those brave kids are worth nothing but respect and appreciation. They stand against your racism, hatred, prejudice, and lousiness. However, I cannot deny that there are still several moderate people who can stand against injustices and face those criminals and cowards who think they are strong by their artillery, helicopters, and war machineries. The Israelis know very well that what they are doing is not a brave act. Otherwise, they would have fought people with the same balance, the same amount of weapons, and the exact same force. They fight people who do not have the least to defend themselves with. Look at the pictures of the poor boys and girls whose heads and bodies were buried under the rubble. Remember the little girl who was being examined for her injury and was crying badly mourning her late mother who was murdered in the same coward Israeli incursion, which she was injured in. Look at the demonstrations all over the world that ask those war criminals to stop but no way to stop them. Look again at Rice and Bush who gave her the order not to vote for the UN resolution to seize fire. The administrations and governments all over the world are asking Israel to stop at the time Bush and Rice give them the green light to continue. Until when can they defy the whole world? Wasn't it enough after their reckless wars against Afghanistan and Iraq? Didn't they learn anything from the previous mistakes? Don't they care how many Americans they sent in harms way and caused them to be killed, amputated, or become handicapped and dependent on others for the rest of their lives?! Will they learn one day? I think it is too late, even if they learn. The world is sick of them, their policies, their arrogance, and their lack of respect towards others, especially Middle Eastern, Arabs, and Muslims.

The best description that I heard about President George W. Bush is that he always has a state of denial and sense of fantasy. Look at Bush, his racist, and prejudiced situations and you will understand what I am speaking of. His fantasizing makes him insist that Iraq is a better place because of him. Just remember the pair of shoes of Zeidi and then tell me how that happened if it is a better place. Why many Iraqis see you as their first enemy, Sheiaa and Sunnis? How is that Mr. President?

I am glad your miserable presidency ended. I am satisfied that I am not going to hear you taking a major decision that can influence the whole world anymore. It is great you are leaving the White House, which I believe; you should have never stepped inside in the first place. It is neither your place nor the right position for you. You refused to meet Arafat and never treated him as a president. You do the same to Ahmedi Najad and not allow him to move in the United States, just in the United Nations. This is not right Mr. President, neither from you nor from any other president or politician who will take the same position and stand.

One of the assertions that President Bush sees things the way he loves and wants them to be is his former Press Secretary Scott McClellan who wrote in his own book that the president made things out of his own spin. Whether I do not agree with McClellan that he had not known that when he was working in the White House, I agree with everything he described about Bush. McClellan was very close to Bush and knows everything about him. Another good and important issue McClellan made was overhearing Bush during his 2000 presidency campaign stating that he did not remember if he had ever taken and used cocaine or not. I support McClellan's view that is nothing that can be forgotten. It does not make any sense like the situation my former friend Sarah Draper mentioned to me that she did not remember if she voted for Bush or Kerry in 2004. Who can forget such a thing unless he or she got an amnesia or Alzheimer? I also agree with a friend of mine who told me once, "If you lie and keep repeating the same lie, you will eventually believe it." That is what happened with President George W. Bush who believed his own lies, imagination, and dream of becoming a maverick. Look how Bush was always met wherever he went with demonstrations and objections. The peoples' voice in any country represents their feelings towards the visitor. He was always an unwanted visitor and he knew that very well. However, it is no wonder now he still persists that he had done a great job. It was really great in the amount of destruction, hatred, and disrespect.

Gaza is burning and he does not say a word about it, which is better than his great statements. The lands, the fields, the people, the factories, the stores, and the UN foods and human aids are burning in Gaza. What a disaster?! What a miserable situation? What a cruel world that keeps silent behind all these Israeli crimes! It is a real shame and disgrace for the whole world. It is disrespect to the whole world community and the UN. Who gave the Israelis these privileges and made them superior to everyone? They can see themselves the way they want but this does not work for me. I am repeating and assuring it that you Israelis are not superior. You prove to be inferior every day with your lousy, stupid, and unjustified aggression on the helpless poor Palestinians. It is a real war against Palestinians. Israel is trying to wipe Palestinians, then Arabs and Muslims off the earth and the universe. Israel is fond of demolishing every building that can be beneficial to Palestinians. Israel helps spreading death, hunger, ignorance, and hatred. It is more than natural that the Israeli hatred is met with hatred from Palestinians, Arabs, and Muslims who are already fed up with Israel and its lies. Israel and Bush were successful spreading the rumors that Arabs are terrorists. They did a wonderful job influencing other moderate people and turn them to be haters who are full of disrespect towards Arabs. The Israeli killers and terrorists became like a naive innocent child who just defends himself or herself against the aggression? What aggression are you talking about and who is the aggressor? You leave the Israeli aggressors and turn to the people who can hardly find housing, water, food, or work because of Israel's bullies and blame them?! Where is the common sense? What happened to your moderation and neutrality, if you do not want to say the truth and admit that Israel is wrong and it is a dangerous loose gang that practices terrorism and corruption against her hosts, the Palestinians, and her Arab neighbors?

Some of the people who were injured in the Israeli raids against Gaza are Egyptian officers and soldiers who guard and protect the Egyptian borders with Gaza. Look how Israel enjoys her cruelty under a cover of protection from the world leaders who either support her through their propagandas and speeches or keeping silent and standing still, and watching on the lines. Bush, the first maverick is leaving the White House and coming to lie to people that all his decisions were effective, sound, and had to be taken. Admit your mistakes once Mr. Bush. Say you were wrong and arrogant all the time. Shame on you, your administration, and those who supported and voted for you; real shame on all of you! You made him think he is a real hero and that he liberated Iraq. Hell no. He did not. He created violence and hatred among Iraqis. He used the old colonial proverb that says separate people to become their master. You are nobody's master, Bush. You are just your own master. If you were a real master, those who used to be your loyal people and part of your administration would have never endorsed, supported, and voted for Barack Obama. They should have endorsed John McCain then but they know him and you. Colin Powell and Scott McClellan are two of those who exposed your lies, your arrogance, and lack of respect and consideration. You are a liar, a miserable liar who does not even know how to lie and make people believe you. Look at the naive lie you and your intelligence spread during the first days of your war against Iraq. You said you found a mobile lab for the weapons of mass destruction in a truck. Please! Give me break and get off my back. Another shame on you Mr. President, you and your maverick intelligence people!

Once more, to the Americans who say and wonder why others always ask America to take care of their business, I say when America stops supporting Israel against them, degrade them, and show the Arab peoples some respect, then it is alright to agree with what you are requesting. Before that, I cannot agree to your opinion because such a tendency and belief by you is a real double standard. ***Enough Double Standard***.

Israel, besides her attacks on civilians, mosques, and churches also destroys and demolishes the schools, colleges, and universities? In this Gaza war and attacks, why did Israel target the building of the college of Science and Technology? The answer is simple. Israel wants to murder all Arabs and makes the ones whom she cannot kill for some reason very ignorant. In turn, he or she can never be independent. Israel wants to insult and humiliate Arabs and Arabs are supposed to kneel for the maverick state of Israel who came from nowhere. Arabs let them stay in their lands and the cowards are kicking them out of their lands. Why do you idiots target children, the same way you did with the Egyptian primary school of Bahr Al-Bakar? The answer is also simple. Israel finds it easier to kill those poor children in order not to resist her power when they grow up.

How funny that the mighty Israel, with all her military and nuclear power, believe that their end and surrender from the Arab lands will occur by Arab children. No wonder they kill every child they can reach. It does not matter to them if that child is a boy or girl. Israelis suffered from Hitler and the Nazis and they apply what they had suffered from with Palestinians, Arabs, and Muslims with more brutality.

Israel did not leave a Palestinian family without killing at least one of its members. In fact, the family that just lost one person is luckier than most of the families, which had already lost dozens and dozens of their men and women. After all that Israel, you want us to respect you?! Hell no, when you respect yourself first, we then respect you. You do not own our lives or possess our lands. Gaza is Arab. Palestine is Arab. Long live Gaza and Long live Palestine.

Israel killed a 15 year old young man just because he was demonstrating against her intolerant aggressions and practices. Israel assassinated thousands of Palestinians and Arabs as it thinks it owns them, their destiny, their life, their past, present, and future. Israel killed the innocent infants and toddlers. Israel deprived the children of their parents, families, and homes. Israel is an idiot who needs to go to a big lunatic asylum. Israel needs to be separated from the moderate and just world. A traitor like Israel cannot be trusted, respected, loved, listened to, or appreciated. Israel has to be ignored and dumped in a huge garbage dumpster. Again, this has nothing to do with Jews or Judaism. It is just against the cruel, coward, and inhumane practices of Israel.

While the Israeli severe war is still going on its third week, that cruel war cost Palestine 1.4 billiard dollars. Is Israel going to pay for that? Is she going to return those whom she murdered back to life? Is Israel, or the life taker, going to leave Palestinians alone and mind her own damn business? Do you think this can happen one day? I hope so but I doubt it because killing Arabs and annoying them in every possible way is Israel's main business. What will Israel do then if peace prevails? Israel cannot live in peace. Israel has to destroy, kill, terrorize, dehumanize, insult, deprive, shoot, and degrade. Israel cannot respect Palestinians because they ask for the simplest rights of a good life, respect, prayers, integrity, and humanity. Are these requests unreasonable? Why do you think Palestinians cannot have their rights like every other nation or people? Palestine should be noticed again as a sovereign country as it was before its usurpation in 1948. Israel has to recognize people's right, respect the moderate world, and submit to the UN Security Council's resolution. Israel has to know she is not exceptional, no matter what George W. Bush had told them, praised them, and promised those several privileges they do not have the simplest right in one of them.

Imagine when 20.000.00 homes and apartment buildings in Gaza were demolished or partly destroyed. Suppose this happen to the home or apartment of one of us, can he or she still praise Israel and agree with Bush in his racism and prejudice against Arabs? Let's put ourselves in the Palestinians shoes before we make ourselves judges. Please also note these numbers are taking place and effect while the Israeli unjustified war is still going on. That is why the UN Secretary General described such a war as an unprecedented disaster. Israel should be kicked out from the UN membership. This is the least that can be taken against her because of her continual disrespect to the Security Council's resolutions. It is not just that. I am repeating and assuring that Israel always targets the UN schools, locations, human aids, and trucks with their drivers. How come it is still a member in the UN?!

THE ISRAELI CONTINUAL DOUBLE STANDARD

What is the difference between the massacres of Gaza and Lebanon in which Israel killed the innocent children, women, and elderly people and those of the Nazis towards the Jews? The difference is simple. Israel is always showing herself as a victim to rip the world. Look how it always makes the Germans feel sorry for her. Look at them again, and I am saying and repeating it. Consider again how the Israelis met Pope John Paul the second with the sign that the swastika equals the cross. They are wrong because the swastika equals the David Star drawn on the Israeli flag. They want the whole world to feel sorry and sad for them ultimately. Henceforth, the world pays and keeps paying them for something most of the people have nothing to do with.

With all what they get from the world from money, support, and sympathy, the Israelis meet that with aggression and hatred towards Palestinians. The Israeli Foreign Minister Tzipni Livni keeps talking about another possible war or wars against Gaza. What the hell she wants? Why doesn't she find something else to talk about? Why doesn't she find herself a video game through which she can practice killing targets and shooting at them instead of targeting and killing real people? People are not your puppets or targets woman. Leave people alone and mind your own damn business. Find yourself some real promises for your people if you want to win the election and become the next Israeli Prime Minister.

HOLOCAUST OR NO HOLOCAUST?

Today is Wednesday, February 04, 2009. The Vatican issued a statement demanding a person who denied the holocaust to concede and reconsider his position. How many years had passed after the "holocaust?" Why should people keep mentioning the "holocaust," cry for it, and show their sorrow for the Maverick Israeli state? Why don't the officials tell Israelis not to practice their killing and corruption on earth? Several moderate Jews refuse the Israeli practice. I support and thank them for their brave and honest position and attitude towards the state of Israel and its cruel and reckless leaders.

Furthermore, should a bishop be denied a position because he revealed his real feelings towards the "holocaust?" Didn't the officials see or hear about the other Maverick who invented the apple story and wrote a whole book about it? Didn't they see how it was an impossible story that his wife went every day to him to the concentration camp and gave him an apple? Didn't they hear the confession of that Maverick writer that he lied and invited that story? He finally after several years of lying had to admit he was falsifying his story to have and publish a novel. He was trying to attract a great deal of attention to his book, which was or is, still to be converted to a movie soon. How is it easy to tell lies? Look at the double standard of the world that chooses willingly to believe such lies and myths. It is the same world who sees Israel and its war actions then defends it. Why won't we doubt the "holocaust" if we see the lies of the Israelis every day on cable TV and the lies of this writer in the Oprah Winfrey show? If the world keeps supporting lies and liars, what should the world expect? More lies, of course. Additionally, the world then should expect more demands, threatening from bullies and liars.

Moreover, why does the Israeli president, prime minister, ministers, officials have the right to criticize others anywhere in the world, deny their beliefs, and show their sarcasm towards them at the time others are denied such a right? Isn't this a double standard? The blind support of George W. Bush to Israel and his actions helped a great deal make the Israeli officials proud of themselves, their murders, and war actions. Enough double standard and don't hurt your own people, employees, and subordinates just for the sake of pleasing Israel. Do not block people's right to express themselves. Help people to see the truth. Do not force people to see facts according to the Bush's and the Israelis' way. Support the right action and do not hinder an opposing view. I know well and understand that Pope Benedict XVI came from Germany. Even if Pope Benedict XVI believes in the holocaust or says it is true because he is originally from Germany, this does not mean he should deny the bishop a position or a rank in the Vatican because he has a certain vision of that "holocaust" and denies it. Why should he be forced to say it is true? Why shouldn't we admit the Israeli massacres, in this age of technology, satellites, Internet, and cable TVs is true? We did not see live pictures of that "holocaust" on TV. We saw the Israeli war actions and practices. We saw the Israelis preventing TV announcers, photographers, and producers from coming near their war zones in Gaza under the pretence of their protection, security, and safety. At the same time, the German Chancellor, Angela Merkel sent Pope Benedict XVI to make a statement that shows rejection to the denial of Bishop Richard Williams. Who asks an Israeli official or even a regular Israeli citizen to recant anything he or she says, shows, expresses, or believes in? ***Why the Double Standard here?***

Bishop Williamson statement came in a Swedish TV interview in which he stated that history and historical facts do not support that 6 million Jews died in the holocaust. The bishop expressed his feelings and how he sees the holocaust. Why do we blame him for his view and interpretation for the holocaust? Let him express himself and do not build fences and barbed wires around people to intimidate them. Bishop Williamson is entitled to his own opinion. Do people have to be hypocrite in order to be respected and appointed in the jobs and positions they deserve? What a cruel world that punishes the honest people and applaud to the criminal state of Israel! Williamson issued an apology to the pope for his remarks because they created controversy and because the pope was born in Germany. That was not enough. They still wanted him to regret his statement about the holocaust.

Why do I have to agree with you about something I do not believe in? Why do you force your opinion on me? Where is democracy then? Where is the understanding and appreciation for others' feelings and beliefs? Do we all have to support and applaud for Israel all the time at the time Israel shows us all the contempt and lack of appreciation and consideration?

THE CONTINUAL ISRAELI LIES
ABOUT THE GAZA WAR

Israeli officials keep lying that the motives of their war against Gaza were the protection of Israel and the Israeli citizen. It is obvious that many Israeli citizens are happy, believe such lies of their leaders, and support them by saying they are brave and not scared. What bravery is that, the bravery of killing and destruction?! Ehud Barack said their actions are like TV reality shows. I agree with you Barack that it is a reality show that shows your lies, wickedness, and brutality, you reckless bloody handed butcher.

Reports say that the three main competent in the coming Israeli elections are the former official and Prime Minister Benjamin Netanyahu, the current Defense Minister Ehud Barack, and the current Foreign Minister Tzipi Livni. The three of them show their aggression and hatred in order to win the position of the next Israeli Prime Minister. The one who shows and approves to be the most dangerous killer and aggressor is the one who will win this election. Look at the Israelis' standard of choice of their leaders. The people who keep crying about the "holocaust" executed and still execute numberless holocausts against Palestinians every day. Whenever the number of the victims increases, the applaud spreads.

The Israeli officials are lying about the ugly and nasty way they treat Palestinians. What about all the Palestinian prisoners who are detained without a crime for indefinite times without trials exactly like the prisoners held in Guantanamo Bay by Bush and his cruel administration and officials who did not care the least about the simplest human rights and who also pretended that those are not considered prisoners of wars so they cannot be treated as prisoners of wars. In turn, Bush and the Israeli officials applied the laws of the jungle on their innocent prisoners. It was alright for them to hold people without charge, to deprive people of their families, and deprive their families and loved ones from them. It did not matter to them to have their children grow up away from their eyesight, love, care, and attention. The Bush and the Israeli administrations perceived themselves as the Lord of the Universe who controls people's life and death. They are both experts at humiliation and disrespect.

To the readers who do not like what they are reading, be patient before you make a judgment and say there are no revelations and it is all complaints about mistreatment and racism. What revelations more than that you want? I am revealing to you the rudeness of the Bush and the Israeli administrations. If you do not see their practices the way I describe them, it is your business. If you are not open minded and see how they crossed all the red line, then have a great time and enjoy commending Bush and the Israeli officials for their cruelty, inhumanity, rudeness, recklessness, and lack of vision.

Neither Bush nor the Israeli officials knows the least about politics. They understand a great deal about destruction and murders. They are butchers who think they own the lives of every human being. They think it is alright to give orders to strike a building killing dozens of people because they are targeting one single person inside the building. They think that people have to believe their false statements and devastating intelligence information, which usually prove to be false and fake like them. They assure their racism and hatred to other people. No wonder how Bush did a great job weakening the Muslim and the Arab World a great deal to please the Israeli leaders. No wonder he was a maverick in ignorance in his continual ignorance to Arafat. No wonder he saw Sharon as a man of peace as he exactly sees himself. The most two destructive people made themselves men of peace. Who are the men of war then, if not Bush, Sharon, and the current Israeli leaders?! Again, I say, write, and repeat it; I blame those who reelected Bush more than Bush himself and his administration. I blame ignorance, hatred, and racism. I blame prejudice and disrespect. I blame those who serve the Israeli goal of extending and enlarging Israel at the expense of Arabs just because they were brought up to hate Arabs. I blame the wrong teachings, the stubbornness, and stereotypes. I blame the mavericks who insist that Arabs are camel jockeys who know nothing about civilization and modern life.

Consider how, when, and where civilization started. The first civilization began in Egypt 7000 years ago. Egypt taught the whole world everything: Medicine, engineering, agriculture, architecture, and sciences. Civilization started from the East, the Muslim and Arab World. As the Egyptian civilization, there was the Iraqi and Yemeni civilization that also enlightened the world. I admit you are more advanced now but this does not mean you accuse others of ignorance, backwardness, and terrorism. The disrespect you show towards Arabs directly and indirectly is not appreciated or respected. However, I still have some more little respect to those who show me hatred in my face. I experienced and saw others who are nice in my face or in the face of the other Arabs. Then, behind their back, they say, "I don't like him," "I don't like her," and "I don't like them." This is still better than those who say 'hate' instead of 'don't like.'

THE CONTINUAL DISCUSSIONS OF 9/11

efore you accuse Arabs of the 9/11 attacks, accuse George W. Bush, Dick Cheney, and their administrators. They insist they made America safer. How come they did that if America was attacked during their era? I still blame those who gave them their trust and made them think they are mavericks and unprecedented. I accuse those who did not vote for John Kerry of being reckless, stubborn, and easy to deceive. I tell them again to enjoy their glorious choice of Bush and Cheney. It is true that neither Bush nor Cheney is in office now. However, consider how many years or decades it will take to fix the devastating mess they had made and caused America and the whole world. Enjoy your choice mavericks and sing for it. We should compose a song for you too for your sound choice. Have fun with your magnificent brilliancy.

You have chosen a person who did not work for peace and stability. Bush should have been moderate, impartial, and nonpartisan in the method he dealt with Israel and the Israeli leaders. The world leaders should increase safety, security, and public awareness. They need to work for increasing food production and create more understanding between the different nations. In the case of Bush and the Israeli leaders, they did nothing but the opposite. Bush and the Israeli leaders are just good at the policy of threatening, burning, and demolishing. They do not use their minds but their muscles. They do not listen to the sound of wisdom but to the sound of arrogance and false pride. They did not help the weak people to get over some of their troubles. They made them weaker and weaker. Look at Bush directly after the end of his era. Compare the amount of job losses nowadays. It is the worst since 1976. Bravo President Bush. Bravo Dick Cheney. Well done guys. ***Great job!***

The world leaders should set a good example for the youth of their counties in love, respect, mercy, humanity, and forgiveness. Bush and the Israeli leaders set excellent examples in hatred, disrespect, lack of mercy, inhumanity, and unjustified and imbalanced retributions. It does not hurt also to set an example in adventures but good adventures, not adventures that kill and destruct. The Victorious George W. Bush gave one of those unappreciated adventures by going to war in Iraq. He never cared the least about any single human soul, including those of the American soldiers, administrators, and civilian employees who went to work in Iraq. The same applies to the continual governments and administrations of Israel. However and to be impartial, as I had mentioned in previous publications, I have to give Menachem Begin and Yitzhak Rabin credit for their peace efforts and endeavors.

Menachem Begin, the former Israeli Prime Minister worked for peace with the late Egyptian President Anwar Sadat. They were brave men who were not scared of the opinions of their critics from both sides. They saw the right path and went through it. They both believed strongly that saving a single human life is greater than throwing the soldiers of both countries in harms way. They achieved peace with the help and coordination of the American President then, President Jimmy Carter. Just think with me if President George W. Bush was the American President then, would peace between Egypt and Israel be achieved? Of course not, how could peace prevail with Bush who works for the destruction of humanity and life loss other than being a life savior. It does not matter to Bush as the life loss is far from him and his loved ones. Can you see the selfishness? Can you tell how Bush did his best to make history? He made history but heinous history, which is no different from the history of Adolf Hitler. Bush's vivid imagination made him convince Americans that Arabs and Muslims hate America. He went on his way of killing civilians without any regard of their relatives' feelings. He did not give a second thought about those who were going to become widows, orphans, handicapped, or disfigured.

If we also compare between Menachem Begin and current Israeli *Mavericks*, we will find a great difference. The peace agreement between Egypt and Israel was reached just a few months after Menachem Begin took office. See how he was a brave peaceful man and how the current ones are dishonest liars. Look how other Israeli leaders acted like Bush or Bush acted like them, it does not matter as both have the same greedy thinking. Israel invaded and occupied Lebanon and Bush did the same with Iraq. If you are going to say it is to help Iraq, go back to the statement of Cindy Sheehan who exposed the lies of George W. Bush. Sheehan assured us that her son died while guarding a well of oil. She believed he died during war actions first but then she found out the truth and revealed it. Consider if Ehud Barack, Benjamin Netanyahu, Tzipni Livni, or their current president Shimon Perez were in office as a prime minister in 1977, would Israel and Egypt have reached the Camp David peace treaty? No, it was the successful peaceful triangle of Carter, Sadat, and Begin. Now, we have gangs of terror who know nothing more than killing. This is also the current Israeli leaders' way to get the satisfaction of their people and make them vote for them.

Leaders should teach their peoples to respect the rights of others, not to deprive them of their rights. Bush and the current Israeli leaders deprive people of their simplest rights, which is the right of life. Every person has the right to lead a decent life but those ones do not allow several others just to live, even the worst kind of life. They take their lives with their modern war machines. They believe it is too much to leave others who are humans like them to lead the most miserable and poorest life. They should help them but they kill them instead. Maybe those leaders like Bush and the Israeli leaders have their excuse. They are trying to get over the current world financial crises so they save the world the expenses of the food those poor souls were going to eat and consume. They also save the other resources they were going to consume such as water, electricity, education, and medicine, and oil. See how nice Bush and the Israeli leaders. They are murdering those guys so they and you can enjoy your life and save you some resources others were going to enjoy if they lived. Thank those guys or let me thank them on behalf of you. ***Thanks Bush, you and the Maverick Israeli leaders. Thanks a lot.***

Bush always shows himself as a religious leader and person. Shouldn't a religious leader bring the rights of the poor and oppressed people back to them or leave them alone if he is not willing to assist and support them? Shouldn't a religious leader say nothing if he cannot be impartial? Shouldn't he stay aside other than hurt and devastate the situations of the people who own nothing? Shouldn't he have told the Israeli people to tell their soldiers to treat Palestinians in a human way? Why did he keep lying to us? I saw it many times on TV before Al-Jazeerah, Al-Arabia, or any of those fairly new channels because I know many people are going to say it is because of these Arab TV channels. No, my dears, I saw it years ago before anyone hears about any of these channels. I saw Israeli soldiers kicking kids, tying young people in the army vehicles, and pull them on the roads. Imagine the injuries and scratches they can get from that. Think of what they do with them away from cameras after that. Isn't that a ***'holocaust?'*** Why didn't the leaders of those soldiers teach them to respect the Palestinians? Why did they give them orders to beat them? Why did they allow them to insult Palestinians with the most heinous words and phrases? Why didn't they teach them to respect Palestinians so Palestinians could respect them back? Why didn't they apply the laws that say an occupying force should protect the people of the land they occupy? Why did those leaders allow their officers and soldiers to shoot and kill innocent Palestinians? Why did the lousy soldier kill Mohammed El-Dora and injure his father after kicking them with his military heavy boots? Why cruelty and inhumanity? Why did Bush never show respect to Palestinians? Why did he keep giving Israel what the called ***'the right to defend itself?'*** Why didn't he give a single statement about Palestinians and their right to defend themselves during his eight years of presidency?! ***What a Double Standard!***

The Importance of Moderation

One of my favorite TV programs, which I always watch when I get a chance, is *CNN* Larry King Live. I know very well that Larry King is Jewish. However, as I had mentioned earlier I have nothing against Judaism or Jews. I respect and appreciate them. I also, as you know well, believe in Judaism like all Muslims. I always believe that it is not our business to judge people because of their religion. It is God's business, never ours. I never talk about religion unless someone urges me too. However, I still speak of religions with respect if I got to.

Larry King never sides with one person or party against the other, even if the discussion is about Israel. Mr. King is always patient, attentive, and respectful. I am mentioning that to prove again talking about Israel with its current leaders have nothing to do with their religion. If they are good people, they should do all whatever they can to stop the killing. They should not act like butchers who slaughter others because they differ with them in religion, language, and beliefs. Our faith is between us and God. We should never make ourselves Gods because there is only one God who wants us to be peaceful.

The teachings of religion do not tell Israeli leaders to go and invade Gaza, kill its people, and demolish their houses because there is a competition among Netanyahu, Livini, and Ehud Barack about who is going to be the coming prime minister. This is again the law of the jungle. Larry king has never shown disrespect to someone who criticized Israel, Arabs, America, or any country. Larry is a good example that those Israeli leaders should follow. When they do, several people can respect Israel and its people. Consider before the second Palestinian uprising in 2000, how conditions were improving. Then, with the coming of Ariel Sharon, things got worse and worse at the hands of that butcher. Sharon found it hard to leave Israelis and Palestinians live in peace. Sharon played the racist card with Arafat. Sharon proved to be one of the most racist people the world had ever seen or known. My advice to the world leaders is not to help their people become like Bush or Sharon. Make your people take the steps of peaceful presidents and leaders like Carter, Sadat, and Begin.

One of the nice incidents I remember after the signing of the peace treaty between Egypt and Israel, an Egyptian citizen and his wife got three new born male babies, they named them after the three leaders: Carter, Sadat, and Begin. See how nice it is when people work for peace. If they were working for destruction like Bush and Sharon or the current Israeli leaders, those two Egyptian married couple would have thought about it one million time before giving their three boys such names. If they had given them those names and those leaders were warmongers, all the people they know would have never supported or appreciated that for them for the rest of their lives. Most of the people like those names because they are names of people who made a good difference in their lives. See how people avoid a person with the name of Hitler. Imagine one of the most Egyptian top officials who was about to be appointed many times in higher positions such as an ambassador or minister. The only reason he was never appointed in any of those major position was his name. He committed no crime but his name is Hitler. Away from his name, I always thought that man should have been in a more important position. He is the former Egyptian general, Hitler Tantawy. The man never committed a crime or hurt anybody. It is just his name. However, I believe we should never blame people for the names their parents had chosen for them. We should never hate someone because his name is similar to someone we hate or someone who hurt us before. The main point here is that people like Bush and those Israeli leaders might hurt others in the future because they have similar names. Therefore, they hurt people directly and indirectly as long as this life continues. How bad is that? What have those done to pay for something they do not have the least to do with?!

Again, it is now the role of President Obama, Vice President Joe Biden, Secretary of State Hillary Clinton to help the American people and the rest of the world to forget about the cruel practices of their predecessors George W. Bush, Dick Cheney, and Condoleezza Rice. The world is fed up with those last three and does not need any more of them. The role of the new administration is to help spread peace and make people forget a little about the Bush unjustified wars against Afghanistan and Iraq. The current administration needs to make people feel more secure and not wiretapped as what Bush had done to them. The administration needs to assure people that it respects their privacy, humanity, and rights. This way, the administration can achieve stability and comfort in the United States. In turn, the American people retrieve their nice and peaceful nature with the outside world. Then, harmony can be restored.

ISRAEL AFTER THE GAZA WAR

Officials said the war is ended but Israel continues to target the Palestinians in Gaza. Moreover, Israel is acting as a pirate. Israel attacked a Lebanese ship sailing in Gaza, kept its crew, insulted, and mistreated them? Why not, if Israel with its leaders always does the same thing of attacking civilians, forbidding people from gaining the necessities of their living, and killing innocents most of the time, or sending them to its inhuman jails and prisons? Some Lebanese appealed and sent a complaint to the UN Security Council. However, we both know that nothing and nobody can stop the Maverick Israel. Could the Security Council force Israel to seize fire?! Israel continued killing, destroying, and demolishing for a long time after the UN resolution. It is no wonder Israel keeps corrupting on earth then under the continual pretence and excuse that Israel has the right to defend itself but the others do not have the simplest rights even to be respected while being held or investigated by Israel.

THE ISRAELI ELECTIONS

Today is Tuesday, February 10, 2009. The Israeli voters all over Israel went to vote. The expectation is either Netanyahu or Livni will take office and become the next Israeli Prime Minister. Netanyahu was in the front and won lots of votes because of his brutality and aggression against Palestinians. Livni is about to bridge the gap and win more votes that can make her the winner. This is because, according to Israelis, Livni is brave because she did her best and made several harsh and hateful statements against Palestinians. The is the measurement of the Israeli voters who are torn between Netanyahu and Livni as both of them are mavericks who spare no efforts to kill Palestinians, destroy their crops and plants, and demolish their houses.

The Israeli mavericks left Palestinians without aids. They left them with no food, no clean water, nor electricity. That is why, after all the splendid efforts of Livni in the past Gaza war and the long wonderful history of Netanyahu in aggression and hatefulness, Israeli voters will be happy with either one. Netanyahu used to give racist and meaningless statements when an Arab army had some military training, saying Arabs are training to attack Israel. The maverick wants to prevent others to be ready to defend themselves. The other maverick, Livni was blaming Fouad Siniora, the Lebanese Prime Minister for all the damages, killing, and destruction her army caused in Lebanon in 2006. They always do the destruction and kill people collectively then cry about the 'holocaust.' Livni was telling Siniora to prevent his people from defending themselves against the Israeli aggression. Look at that, guys. See how a person or people should stand still while others are attacking them with their heavy war machinery. Look at the people who bomb Lebanon and attack it from the air, sea, and land. Look and consider how it is to attack a country that did not have a single military airplane. Look at the lack of balance, as it is always the case, between Israel the aggressor, and the aggressed. I am asking those voters to think about the mavericks they choose to rule them and control their life and future. Does religion ask you to support the brutality of your leaders? Does religion and ethics tell you to kill Arabs and look down on them? Ask yourselves how many people do not like or hate, Israel. It is because of your severe practices, racism, and aggressions. It is because you are fond of building new settlements in other people's lands. You kick people out of their homes and leave their children fatherless and motherless, if you got some mercy not to kill those children with their parents. However, you torment them both ways. If you kill them, you deprive them of their right to live when they are still in the very best years of their life. Instead of giving them hope in a better future, you steal every hope and good wish from them. Instead of helping them to think about a glorious future, you make their concern how to drink a clean glass of water and have enough food for the day or even just for the coming meal. Don't you think those Palestinians deserve a better treatment? Why don't you see them as human beings and treat their children with respect the way you like to be treated? We learn to treat others the way we like to be treated. You treat them like trash and expect them to throw flowers at you. You are wrong. Why do you wonder and complain when they throw stones at you? Put yourselves in others' shoes before you say your racist comments and make your usual statements that Arabs hate Jews and like to destroy them. You are absolutely wrong. Arabs hate nobody. Arabs love people. Arabs treat people with respect when others respect them. Arabs do not accept injustice or hatred. Stop your holocaust against Palestinians and Arabs. Get out of the lands you occupied. Get out of Syria. Get out of Gaza and abide by the United Nations' Resolutions then ask others to love you. You are better than nobody. All people are created equal. Show some concern about the humanity of others. Others are not your slaves. Don't teach your children the policy of hatred. What do you expect when you start teaching your children to look down on Arabs when they start understanding about the world and the surroundings? Don't you think if your teachings to your kids were different, Arabs would have been different too? Love brings love and hatred produces hatred. These are the simplest rules and lessons we learned at school in the first grade. We learned that you are the one who makes others respect or disrespect you. It is a rule of thumb and you know that very well but you just like arguing.

A simple example of hatred is not to allow Palestinians to cross your check points because of your elections except for urgent medical treatment. How about if someone else is in pain but he does not have to have an urgent surgery? Why do you like to keep people in pain? Even if you say you allow those who have to undergo an immediate checkup or operation, who will believe you and you are the ones who target the Palestinian ambulances, murder their drivers, patients, and those who are injured in your disproportioned war against them?! Who will believe you and you are the ones who target the United Nations' aid trucks, kill the drivers, and burn the aids?! Who will believe you and you are the ones who target the shelters of the United Nations that are supposed to be for the protection of the innocent civilian Palestinians?! Who can trust you after all that? Who can trust liars and hypocrites?! Again, stop crying and talking about the holocaust.

Consider how many holocausts you committed and still commit every day and every hour? Have some common sense. Have some consideration for peoples' lives. You do not own people's souls to kill them the time and the moment you want.

Count with me how many people you killed. Remember Sheikh Ahmed Yaseen? How in the world you kill an 80 year old man and his two sons while returning to their house after praying the dawn in a mosque? Remember Dr. Abdel Aziz El-Rantisi, Ismail Abu Shanab, Salah Shehaza, and others? If I keep writing and mentioning names you murdered, I will need volumes. These are just examples of your brutality and inhumanity. Why do you target people and then blame them when they retaliate? Why do you see Palestinians as terrorists? Palestinians are peaceful people. They are desperate. They do not ask for too much. They ask for peace, food, and water. Are you working on a long term family planning project? Therefore you kill Palestinians? Are you trying to save some resources and money so you attack those poor people? Do you think those Palestinians are the ones who committed the 'holocaust,' so you spare no effort to humiliate them?! I understand if you do not like something you experienced, do not practice it with others.

On Wednesday 11th February, Israeli officials announced that Kadima party and Likud won the elections as their members got several seats in the parliament. As I wrote the day before, I expected the two mavericks of the two parties, Livni and Netanyahu to win because of their clear brutality, aggressiveness towards Arabs, and the intelligence like their predecessor Ariel Sharon. That is when they invent and create violence and instability to postpone the execution of their peace treaties and agreements because they have to surrender from a piece of land they had occupied. The occupiers do that. In turn, the treaty is put off to an indefinite period of time, which means it is postponed forever. This is an explanation for the guys who do not know what is going on between Israelis and Palestinians and who wonder why Palestinians feel desperate. Do you think they can feel hopeful and happy in such miserable situations and inhumane conditions? Who can tolerate that? Put yourselves in their positions then tell me if you can handle such a lousy treatment and indifference.

The Israeli officials were kind hearted enough to allow some Palestinians in Gaza to export some of their flowers in Valentine's Day. The Palestinians who grow these flowers said that was nothing because they were allowed to export few thousands of these followers at the time they could export millions of them. See how the Israeli officials are nice. They did not destroy these flowers for the Palestinians. They help them to make use of their stuff. Oh yeah! That is true. They do not make them suffer by turning everything upside down over their heads. Those Israeli officials act like 'the boy who cried wolf.' The boy kept lying until the point no one believed him when he was serious. Can you believe a person who does and says nothing but lies? Think of those you might meet in your daily life, telling you lies to get your money, like that woman, who used to come and tell people that her money was stolen and she has no way to buy gas. A second time, she says her car stopped and she does not ask someone to help her start the car. No, she asks someone to give her money so she can get the car fixed. A third time, "the car is stuck in the middle of the road and we need some money to go to Livonia." That woman used to stay for a while in a certain place. Every time she comes with a different look, accent, and story. She still appears every once in a while with a brand new look. One time appears blonde, which I believe she really is, another with a bun and red head, a third time as brunette, a fourth time covering her head and all her body lying and saying she is a Muslim woman. What I found out indirectly, when I remembered such a woman, that she goes and beg people too in front of the places of worship. It is not just that, she is always ready to lie to each group and convince them that she follows and embraces their religion. She learns by heart words those groups of people say. When she goes there, she tells them about her miserable stories. People feel sorry for her and help her the way they can. She deceived me and other people in front of me. I did not recognize at first that she was the same woman I helped before but she reminded me with herself. The first time she made me pay for her gas and told me her pants were ripped off. I gave her my leather jacket, which I had with me by chance that day to cover herself. She promised to return me the jacket and the money the same day. When she appeared the second time, she was completely different but she told me that I had helped her 9 months ago. Then, I remembered her. I never got my jacket or money back. After that, she still came to my workplace. All what I could do is to warn the people who feel sorry for her and try to help her. I like people to help one another but it is hateful when we see a woman like that, a parasite, who just likes to steal people and get their money. She lives the easy way like thieves and robbers who are so damn lazy to work or do something useful in their life. The goal of mentioning that real story is to assure the damage lying does and causes. A woman like that makes it hard for us, and maybe impossible, to believe others who might be honest and in dire need of money. However, I myself because of this woman and lousy dishonest people like her, I do not help someone if I have a doubt that he or she is lying and trying to take advantage of me. Unfortunately, because there is no law to arrest or persecute this woman and people like her, they go comfortably committing their crimes. Moreover, some people blame that on nice people telling them it was their fault to get fooled by such people. Such statements also make me think one million time before offering a helping hand to someone I do not know who asks for help. I am not happy with that but I do not want to be a fool too.

The Israeli leaders made me unable to believe a single word they say because of their continual lies, their 'security meetings' with the Palestinians, which are supposed to be meetings to execute their treaties, their creation of instability in every possible and impossible way to get out of their promises, and their intolerant and inhumane way of dealing with the Palestinians. The Israeli officials do not have the least respect towards the Palestinian leaders and I don't blame those Palestinian leaders for that. The Israeli leaders inherited this bad habit since the occupation of

Palestine and the formation of Israel in 1948. They believe Palestinians are their slaves. That is why they kill them because they do not kneel and beg Israeli officials and soldiers to have mercy on them. Mercy comes from God and complaint to people is a real humiliation. God is the merciful who forgives us for our wicked deeds and disobedience. However, God did not ask the strong to attack the weak. God never asked us to act like a bunch of wild beasts that live in a jungle or like bigger fishes, which eat the smaller ones. The world is taking the sidelines as usual especially when it comes to Israel. See again how the Israeli mavericks get happy anytime there is an attack on an Arab soil. Consider again how the cowardly acts of George W. Bush against Arabs and Muslims were in the favor of Israel and no one else. Bush made himself seems as if he was receiving his orders from Israeli leaders like Sharon, Olmert, and Livni.

Two personal Memories

One day, I was working in one of my previous jobs. I found my boss, who was also the owner of the business telling me that an old lady was stranded outside and needed some help with her car. Her car needed all kinds of oil, antifreeze, windshield liquid...etc. I said I will definitely help her. I was working in the pizza place next door to the gas station, which was also owned by the same man. The lady was there with the owner. She became impatient and I told her more than once that I was going to help her as soon as I gave those customers their orders as they were waiting for me to finish their sandwiches, salads, and pizzas. I also had to watch the oven so the stuff inside does not get burnt or fall down on the floor as the oven was old and it did not have an edge to prevent the food from falling down when the belt moves. Anyway, she told me after about four minutes exactly that she did not ask for help for free and she was going to pay me. I explained to the lady that I did not want or expect any money from her. I told her again to look around and be patient as these customers were waiting for me before her arrival and they wanted to be served too. She kept murmuring and I respected her because of two things, being a lady and her old age.

As soon as I finished, I went out with her to her car. She ordered me to open the hood then check all the fluids, to measure the tire pressures, and I was more than patient because of the two previous reasons I just mentioned above. I just got curious because of the disgusting manner she was talking to me with. I asked her where she was from as she had a strong accent too. She assured me she would tell me as soon as I finish my job. She made my help for her a job or something I was obliged to do. When we were done, she asked me if I am Arab and I answered yes. She said I am from your country. Then, I asked her which country she was talking about. She asked me if I was Palestinian. She did not wait for my answer. She told me she was Israeli and opened her car door, started it, and drove without even saying thank you. I am not a person who expects people to thank me when I am able to help them. As I always say and repeat, I just like the people to treat me the way I treat them. If I had known she was Israeli before I helped her, I would have still helped her and that would have made me no difference at all. I am not the one who likes to be judgmental towards others. If I hate the behavior of the continual Israeli governments, I do not hate the Israeli people. However, I do not support those who say publicly that they hate Arabs and Muslims. Why will I do that?!

Another important thing I like to say, if that lady had told me she was Israeli at the beginning and acted that rude, the way she acted and talked to me, I might have not helped her at all. This is because that would seem like an announcement of disrespect because I am Arab. She was acting as if Arabs are her slaves who have to listen to her commands. It was good she did not have a whip with her when she was telling me to do what she wanted in her car. I am saying this to explain to you that the belief you might have that Islam is a religion of violence is a false one and those who spread such rumors are nothing but haters. Islam has never been violent.

The assumption that Muslims are terrorists is a rude and incorrect one. Muslims do not commit state terrorism like the Israeli leaders who practice that kind of terrorism against Palestinians day and night. The Isareali leaders who always give themselves the right to invade others' lands are the terrorists. Those who target the civilians are the aggressors. The people who use their heavy artillery are the violent, who create and produce more violence. The ones, who attack people and always expect them to surrender, kneel, and cry, are the cowards. The persons who kill infants and toddlers are the ruthless.

The second memory was not a happier one. It occurred a few months after the first one. I was distributing pizza fliers. The rule I know is that when I see a "No soliciting" Sign, I just keep going to the next house and so on. Therefore, I never put a flyer at a door that has such a sign or a similar one. Moreover, if I see someone in front of or around a house, I ask him or her if I can hand him a flyer. So, it is really up to them. That guy I am going to tell you about happened to be sitting inside his house in that day, which was a Saturday. I did not see him as I never try to look inside people's houses because I respect peoples' rights and privacy. He waited until I put a flyer outside his door and started walking away. Then, I heard a voice. It was him. He opened his door and told me he does not need my flyer. He said it in a very lousy ugly manner, which was void of any kind of respect. I said no problem and walked back towards him to recollect my flyer. He threw it on the ground and ordered me to pick it up. Honestly, if I was not experiencing very hard times then in terms of money, I would have acted differently. I would have insulted him back because this was not act of a decent man. I got so nervous and started losing my temper and he insisted that I pick the flyer up. Finally, I did and walked away from him. I am mentioning this situation again because of one more important thing. It was not just the financial problems that made me abide and pick the flyer up. It was my religion. That was my first motive to act wisely and patiently. God orders us in Qur'an, our holy book to be patient, to hide and control our anger, and to forgive people. I am a Muslim and he is a Jew. How did I know? From his Yakama, the Jewish small round hat he was wearing atop his head that Saturday. Besides acting wisely because of religion, I acted that way again and God's orders and instruction were my motive to be polite with that person. If I had acted differently, I would have given a bad picture and impression about Islam and Muslims. I was so impatient inside because I could do nothing with my degrees and certificates in the United States. I thought people in the states are always moderate, nice, and wise. I believed they apply what they write and type on every job application that they do not discriminate on basis of religion, color, race, or ethnicity. I found out that written words, phrases, and statements on job applications are something and the reality is something else. I got stuck on pizza and restaurant jobs. In fact, I experienced sometimes during which I could have no job at all. Several people told me that I was humiliating myself in such jobs. However, this is what I could get from such people. If I ask them if they have a substitute, the answer is always, "That is America man." What an accurate answer! I tell these people if this is America, they should mind their own business because their inquiries, criticism, and sarcasm do not help at all. They make people's life impossible with their unjustified interference in their lives. They add to people's misery. People are already miserable so get off their backs. If you can find them a better job, that is wonderful. If not again, get out of their way and let them live their life.

Following God's orders in my response to that person was very reasonable. It was the only thing I could do. As I had mentioned, I am not a person who gives a bad picture about his religion. I would have made it worse too if I responded to him in an ugly manner, which matches his disgusting attitude, intolerance, and racism. If I had behaved like that hateful one, who was not taught manners or brought up properly, I might have been fired from my job. Then, I would not be able to handle my bills, food, daily expenses, and all the costs of living. Had I listened to those who advised me to quit such jobs, none of them would have helped me with a penny. They would tell me, "This is America man!" Then, the only solution in order not to starve and die is to go begging. Islam also tells us that any honest job a person can do is better than begging. Islam is also against crimes and I am not the one who goes stealing even if it costs me my life. I am not that one. I apply the teachings of Islam, which say a Muslim has to respect people's property and do not try to take anything that do not belong to him or her. Look at the Israeli leaders who usurped the land, demolished the houses, and ended people's lives. Isn't that stealing? Isn't that highway robbery? Isn't that terrorism? If not, what is it then?!

Those people who interfere in others' business remind me of a friend of mine who experienced a similar situation. He worked with me in that fast food restaurant. There was that man who used to come and buy lunch from that restaurant. The man used to tell my friend that he should not be doing that job and that any boy could do that. One day, my fried got angry at him and asked him if he had a better job for him. The man told him the same famous sentence, "This is America man." My friend got angrier and advised him to leave him alone then. He also said to him, "When you pay my bills, rent, and expenses, you can blame me for that job and then I will listen to you."

Had that Jewish man acted with me the way several Jewish and Israelis call themselves, 'the chosen people of God on earth,' he would have shown me some little respect, he would have handed me the flyer in my hand, he would not have shown satisfaction in making me kneel in front of him to pick up the flyer from the ground. What an ugly man he is! How easy to be rude and reckless! Nothing in the world is easier than that. Look at the Israeli leaders and see how they treat Palestinians and you will know how ugliness can be easy. However, it is not easy for every one. See how George W. Bush dealt with the Muslim world and you can tell what ugliness can reach when a leader like Bush hates certain people. Consider how many approvals Bush gave Israelis to go on their way of hatred and aggression against Muslims. Remember how Bush accumulated accusations towards Arabs and Muslims.

Besides all that, consider the conspiracy theory and all the opinions that say that Bush had benefits in September 11 to go to Afghanistan and Iraq. Afghanistan is a gate to Asia and Iraq is a gate to the Middle East with its oil and resources. Consider how several politicians act and do anything to get away with what they want. I still remember Dr. Yunnan Labib Rizk, my history professor in Cairo University. What a good and brave man he was who taught me and my colleagues a lot about history and politics! He told us many times that most of the politicians use this principal: "The ethical politician is a failure." I believe him strongly. Do not believe everything you hear from politicians. Dr. Rizk was also one of the Egyptian members of the committee that helped restore the Egyptian Taba from Israel. Israel occupied Taba as other lands it usurped. Israel tried to deceive the whole world saying Taba is Israeli. With the experience of Dr. Rizk and his colleagues, which I remember one of them, Dr. Mofid Shehab, Egypt restored Taba from Israel. Although my major was English, Dr. Rizk added a great deal to my love of history and social studies. Hence, I believe President Bush and all the Israeli leaders, except for Begin and Rabin, applied that principal and hanged their ethics in the closet before they took office.

The days post September 11, Bush and his administrators started taking advice from the Israeli butcher Ehud Olmert and others who are famous for their brutality. The Israeli mavericks used to give advice that they have special equipments in their planes and their doors are different from others because they suffer from terrorism. Therefore, President Bush accused Arabs of terrorism and assured it with the Israelis who assured that false accusation. Again, if you say there are tapes, videos, or such things that prove Arabs are involved in terrorist acts, I repeat these things have been faked and fabricated by professionals all over the world who work for intelligence and spying agencies. It is not a big deal. It is not a proof of anything. It is nothing, nothing at all. The issue is there are always premade accusations and ready made assumptions about Muslims being terrorists and Arabs if combined by being Muslims makes it worse. Add to that the American devastating picture and way of talking about Arabs and the old hobby of saying Arabs are camel jockeys…etc.

Again, enough double standard because your double standard policies, acts, and behavior are obvious to most of the people all over the world. Restore the good picture of America, America before Bush, Cheney, Rumsfeld, and Rice. Assure people again that America is a land of peace that respect the humanity of everyone, every nation, every ethnicity, race, color, and religion. Show other peoples the respect they deserve and treat people the way you like to be treated. Help the world to forget about the Bush era, which made America look like a monster and even worse. Put the Bush era aside and don't get carried away by him, his supporters, and advocates. Those are no more than a bunch of racist warmongers who are fond of destruction.

GLENN BECK

Tonight is still Valentine's Day. I turned on the TV and it was accidentally on the Fox News channel. I was surprised to see that announcer, Glenn Beck, as I know him an announcer of CNN headline News. Beck is always different in the way he delivers his material and the way he talks to his guests. Tonight, Beck had some chocolates and a jug of M&M. Beck talked about Ahmedi Najad, the Iranian President, and how he called an Iranian Satellite Hope. Beck made an argument that hope is the hope of Iranians and Shiah to have some religious victories... etc. I do not know how he ended up building this argument in a few seconds. It might be the effect of the M&M and the chocolate he was swallowing. I was always surprised that he was on Fox News, and not CNN headline News. However, I believe Fox News matches him a great deal more because of the style he uses introducing his program, his very argumentative nature that leaves no room for the other opinion, his lack of consideration to people's feelings, and his whole character. Hence, it is possible to say that Fox News now has two mavericks: Sean Hanity and Glenn Beck.

The Glenn Beck show tonight is an addition to the double standard issues in America. When it comes to Muslim countries, who think about having a nuclear peaceful program such as Pakistan and Iran, the harsh and unjustified criticism starts. When it comes to Israel, "Israel has the right to defend itself." The interpretations about the Muslim and Arab Worlds are too many. However, most of those who volunteer for such devastating statements about Arabs and Muslims do not know the least about them. They just know the stereotypes they have learned, heard, said, and repeated since they started learning the alphabets. It is unreasonable that anyone can make judgments like that. It is not an acceptable excuse to say 9/11 is what created the problem between America and Muslims. Say that to someone else who might believe your argument but not to me. You did enough producing hatred towards Muslims and Arabs. These people you talk down about show you respect and appreciation. Several Americans who visited Muslim and Arab countries changed their negative opinion about these countries and their peoples. They found out that the American media gives a false picture about those people and their cultures. Do not make people's religion an obstacle on having good relations with them. These people do not impose their religion on you. Consider the first amendment of the constitution of the United States:

> Congress shall make no law respecting an establishment of religion, or prohibiting the free exercise thereof, or abridging the freedom of speech, or of the press, or the right of the people peacefully to assemble, and to petition the government for a redress of grievances (The Bill of Rights, 1879).

What is happening nowadays contradicts the first amendment. A large number of Americans forget about the constitution, the laws, and the rights' of others. They think because President Bush and his administration defied the world, it is alright for them to act the same way. By doing that, they act like the former administration and deny people their rights "to be secure in their persons, houses, papers, and effects, against unreasonable searches and seizures" (Article III, The Bill of Rights, 1789).

The Bush administration forgot all that and made people insecure in the United States and overseas. They captured many people and brought them to the U.S. in cages similar to that used in Zoos for animals. Even the ones in zoos have room for the animals to move freely. Bush and his people put those people in such cages in the planes and delivered them to the States then to Guantanamo Bay in Cuba. Some of them committed suicide because of the inhuman treatment. Others tried to kill themselves but failed. Many of them were proved to be innocent but that cruel administration applied the rule that say "Guilty until proven innocent." They did not offer a single apology to any of those people or their families. How can they get away with that? How can they defy the U.S. constitution and the Geneva Convention and do not be arrested and tried as war criminals? How come they get away with everything they had done?!

Moreover, they did not only seize those persons and treat them in a devastating manner. Let's read together Article VI of the constitution and see if they have done what it says and assures:

> In all criminal prosecutions the accused shall enjoy the right to a speedy and public trial, by an impartial jury of the State and district wherein the crime shall have been committed, which district shall have been previously ascertained by law, and to be informed of the nature and cause of the accusation, to be confronted with the witnesses against him; to have compulsory process for obtaining witnesses in his favor, and to have the assistance of counsel for his defense (The Bill of Rights, 1789).

Did President Bush give those Guantanamo prisoners who were accused of what he and his administration called 'terrorism' the right of a quick trial?! Did they explain to them why they were detained? Did they give them any of their legal rights? Did they treat them as human beings? Did they allow the United Nations' officials and employees to see them and listen to their complaints and problems? Did they allow those officials to see the amount of disrespect they used while dealing with those prisoners? Didn't they know the whole world knew about the inhuman way they used when they moved them to that base in Cuba? Did President Bush and his administration apply any point mentioned in Article VI of the US constitution?!

All the above points are also subjects of questions for the Israeli leaders who treat the Israeli prisoners the same rude and reckless manners? They give themselves the rights to detain any Palestinian, no matter what gender, age, or health condition he or she is experiencing. They deny those prisoners to have attorneys or legal teams that advise them, or even the right to defend themselves. They do not tell them what crime they are accused of.

Speaking of the double standard issues will take volumes to cover every point. The double standard is still clear when it comes to Muslims and Arabs. Consider with me the statement of Admiral Harry B. Harris Jr., the commander of the Guantanamo Bay prison about the suicide of three detainees. Admiral Harris said, "They have no regard for life, neither ours nor their own. I believe this was not an act of desperation, but an act of asymmetrical warfare waged against us" (Risen, 2006).

What kind of life Admiral Harris is referring to here? Does he call the presence of those prisoners in that facility a life? Death is a lot better than such a life. The Admiral is also trying to doubt their motive to end their miserable life in that notorious prison as an act of war against the United States. The best comment I can say about Admiral Harris' statement is that it is an overreaction resulted from September 11. I heard a political analyst today saying that the American people overreacted after 9/11 and I have seen and experienced that myself. It is not a secret to anyone. However, the statement of the Admiral is not an acceptable one. That shows lack of respect towards those prisoners in their life and after their death. Statements like that influenced the American public opinion in a devastating manner and made people support any enemy for Arabs and Muslims. Again, consider the conspiracy theories and all the lies about September 11 and the 15 Saudis whose names were mentioned in the terrorist list that said to have executed the attacks and then, they were found alive working and living in their homeland Saudi Arabia. This reminds me of the fake competitions that take place on TVs and telephones all over the world. These false quizzes ask people to call as many times as they can to increase their winning chances. Of course, nobody wins at all in such competitions and the names they announce as winners are never real names. In the rare chance of having a name that matches a competitor they announced as a winner, they always have an excuse not to give him or her the prize. The Bush administration and intelligence were more intelligent than those competition companies because they choose names of real people who work for airline companies. Unfortunately for the Bush administration and intelligence, the selected 15 persons have nothing to do with September 11.

Moreover, think of the government act of never trying to correct such a false statement. Please, do not accuse people unless you have a proof. Think again how those Saudi Arabians were in their country the whole day of September 11 and how they put their names in the list of those who attacked America. How come they are alive and all those in the planes were dead. Think of all the tons of explosives, which were implanted in the two Twin Towers of the World Trade Center. It is acceptable to overreact after a horrible incident such as September 11. However, it is not reasonable to keep overreacting forever, especially if there is no evidence of such accusations. Furthermore, it is not a wise act to support Israel against Muslims and Arabs all the time because of false beliefs and inherited teachings. You do not have to side with one group against the other. Try to be moderate and neutral if you do not want to respect Arabs. Suppose, as you say, that the terrorists who executed the September 11th attacks, which you could not prove till today are Arabs, it is still not fair to judge all Arabs and pretend they are all terrorists. ***Enough Double Standard!***

 The author is a doctoral student. He is a supporter of human rights' activists and movements. The author rejects all kinds of violence, at a personal or a state level. He believes unjustified and disproportioned wars are forms of terrorism and oppression. The author also thinks judging a whole people of a certain country as extermists or terrroirists is an unacceptable form of stereotypes. The aouthor is always in favor of using sound judgemets before power, guns, artillery, and helicopters. Using this machinery against peoples and countries that have nothing to defend themselves with is never a brave act. Moreover, using militrary forces against civilians and targetting them is a cowardly act.

Printed in the United States
by Baker & Taylor Publisher Services